S0-AFF-894

The School Social Work Toolkit

Hands-On Counseling Activities and Workshops

Alison Varianides

NASW PRESS

**National Association
of Social Workers**
Washington, DC

Jeane W. Anastas, PhD, LMSW
President

Elizabeth J. Clark, PhD, ACSW, MPH
Executive Director

Cheryl Y. Bradley, *Publisher*
John Cassels, *Project Manager and Staff Editor*
Lori J. Holtzinger, *Proofreader and Indexer*

Cover by Eye to Eye Design
Interior design by Electronic Quill
Printed and bound by Victor Graphics

First impression: January 2013

© 2013 by the NASW Press

All rights reserved. No part of this book may be reproduced or transmitted in any form or by any means, electronic or mechanical, including photocopying, recording, or by any information storage and retrieval system, without permission in writing from the publisher.

Printed in the United States of America

ISBN: 978-0-87101-438-2

CONTENTS

ABOUT THE AUTHOR

ALISON VARIANIDES, LCSW, MSW, is a social worker and psychotherapist in private practice in Westchester County, New York. She has extensive experience working with adolescents, adults, and families. She has worked in the New York City Schools as well as the Westchester County Schools as a school social worker, counseling adolescents with learning and emotional difficulties. In addition, she worked in Dallas, Texas, as a school therapist for grades K through 12 and as a substance abuse counselor for adolescents and adults.

Varianides received her BA in psychology from the State University of New York at Albany, where she graduated Phi Beta Kappa and Magna Cum Laude. She received her MSW from New York University, graduating as an LCU Fellow and Merit Scholar for outstanding academic progress and excellent therapeutic work. She also received a Post-Masters Advanced Certificate in working with individuals with autism spectrum disorders from City University of New York, Brooklyn.

Varianides is the founder and executive director of Westchester Psychotherapy, a private group practice located in Westchester County, New York, serving adolescents and adults. She wrote this book in the hope it would help as many school social workers as possible with the daily tasks and struggles facing our school mental health professionals today.

Varianides lives in Westchester County with her husband, Jason. This is her first social work practice book.

Dedicated to my loving husband Jason,
for his support and encouragement along the way

A NOTE ON USAGE

Throughout this book, I deal with the problem of English's lack of a generic singular pronoun by favoring versions of "they." Though still not entirely accepted in formal writing, this usage is common in everyday speech and—unlike the other standard solutions—is not awkward, sexist, or unclear. I have tried to make this book as accessible and down-to-earth as possible. This use of "they" is designed to be in line with that goal, and it is my hope that it will not be an impediment to enjoyment for readers who are used to more formal stylistic choices.

INTRODUCTION

Welcome to *The School Social Work Toolkit.* This book provides you with hands-on activities, workshops, exercises, and programs for all aspects of school social work. Complete with "how-to" and "sample forms" sections, it will help you define your role as a school social worker and hone your clinical skills. The ethical and legal conflicts that school social workers face—including child abuse reporting, confidentiality, suicidality, and bullying—are discussed. The struggle of defining your role as a mental health clinician in an academic setting is also addressed.

I wrote this book for the new social worker entering the schools for the first time and for the seasoned social worker who could benefit from new activities and workshops for their practice. When I started out as a school social worker, I was faced with many challenges. I remember my first week, I was faced with a child abuse case, a potential suicide risk, and a parent who called and said her child was being bullied and refusing to come to school. I had to handle all of these situations not only quickly, but effectively as well. I wanted to make sure I did the right thing by following the school's standards *and* protecting myself as a licensed social worker. I did what any other new social worker would do . . . research! Well, after a rude awakening of finding out that there were very few books or materials to guide me, I decided to take matters into my own hands and create some policies for common situations that school social workers face. I created policies and assessment checklists for suicide risk, homicide risk, and substance usage. I also began creating curriculums and workshops about topics that were relevant to schools. I wish that I had had a manual to teach me about all of the topics vital to being a school social worker. Sure, I had received a top-notch education from one of the best social work schools in the country, but I still found myself in a world of unknowns as a social worker entering the schools. Now I want to share what I have created with you!

I wrote this book as a guide for school social workers and counselors. Please note that any and all of the activities and exercises in this book can be altered to fit the needs of your school. There are sample templates and forms that you can take and adapt to fit the needs of your students.

I thank you for reading my book and hope you enjoy the workshops, groups, and activities as much as I do!

Chapter 1

DEFINING YOUR ROLE AS A SCHOOL SOCIAL WORKER

A s a school social worker, you may find defining your role to be a difficult task. You may have been hired as the first school social worker your school has ever had, or you may have been hired by a school with a team of social workers. You may be the only social worker at the school or the only social worker responsible for covering all the schools in your district. Regardless of what type of school you were hired into, a school social worker's time is very limited. This is why defining your role from your first day on the job is crucial.

The first thing to think about when defining your role is what you do as a school social worker and the reasons you became one. When I was asked what I did for a living at a cocktail party once by a business professional, I said, "I'm a school social worker. I help teachers and administrators ensure the academic, emotional, and professional success of the students I serve." I then added, "I conduct individual and group counseling for high school students, handle crisis interventions and incidents—including child abuse, suicidal ideation, and bullying—and lead professional development and trainings for teachers."

Your definition of your role may be completely different than mine. It is important to think about what it is you want people to think you do. Make sure you know exactly how you want to be perceived. Practice rehearsing what you would say if a person at a cocktail party asked *you* what it is that you do. You want to be able to explain what you do in a clear and comprehensible way. This is especially important when explaining your role to the school professionals you work with. This is discussed later in this chapter.

When defining your role, you want to make sure you serve three areas: (1) the students, (2) the school staff, and (3) yourself. You can't do everything, so you have to set limits. I am going to discuss how to effectively define your role as a school social worker in several steps.

School districts hire school social workers for mainly three reasons: (1) to deliver direct counseling services to students in need and to support teachers in working with difficult students, (2) to serve in an administrative or leadership role and implement school programs, or (3) to do both.

Even if your role is well defined, either by your job title or your job description, you may still benefit from what I have to offer. If you are lucky, you are in a district that has had social workers before or you are part of a team. The school may know exactly what they hired you for and be clear in expressing that to you. For example, the district may have hired you to work specifically with the special education population. However, if you are the only school social worker, chances are that you are going to get referrals for students from the general education population as well. This is where defining your role comes into play.

Although defining your role in a district that already has defined your role may be easier, it still poses challenges. Time management and scheduling are big issues that school social workers face today. You may often wonder how you will fit in all the students you are mandated to see in addition to the other students demanding your time. Don't forget the individualized education plan (IEP) meetings and paperwork that are required of school social workers. I have heard many school social workers tell me that they struggle with time management. Unlike teachers, school social workers don't have assigned class periods. They usually don't get a "prep" time and rarely eat lunch at the same time every day—if they eat it at all. A teacher knows what class they will have every day third period. Although a social worker may have set a personal schedule, if a crisis or meeting comes up, that schedule falls to the back burner. This can cause the school social worker an immense amount of stress.

STEP 1: MAKE A SCHEDULE

Many school social workers will laugh at me when I say what I am about to say: Make a schedule. Some school social workers say that it is impossible to create a counseling schedule because of the many things that will interrupt it. Although interruptions are inevitable, I still emphasize the importance of making a schedule. Know that when you are making the schedule, it will need to be flexible. However, to create some form of continuity and sanity, making a schedule is highly recommended.

TIP: Include lunch time and paperwork time in your schedule so that you are not backing yourself into a corner and never being able to keep up with the schedule. Do not make the schedule so demanding that you are unable to adhere to it.

What should you include on the schedule? This is when you should be thinking about what you do on a daily basis. You may even want to create a list of all your daily duties and responsibilities. Then incorporate them into your schedule. Include your counseling sessions. You may have set times to see students or groups. Include these on the schedule. Leave some time open for unpredictable "emergencies" or "crises," such as a school fight, a bullying incident, a student who needs to see you right away, and so on. Include meetings and committees that you are a part of. Perhaps you teach professional development to teachers on a monthly basis. Include this in your schedule. You may even want to include some prep time for yourself to get ready. If you find that you can't fit everything you do on a daily basis in your schedule, then you are probably doing too much! Remember, you can't help anyone if you are overworked and stressed out all the time. Creating the schedule is a great way to help you set limits for yourself.

STEP 2: COMMUNICATE YOUR SCHEDULE

Now that you have made a schedule to help you define your role as a social worker by what you do on a daily basis, you have to communicate it to others. Give a copy of your schedule to teachers, administrators, and other school staff. Talk to your students about when their counseling sessions will be and when your "free" time is. Also, explain to students about the need for flexibility. Although it says on your schedule that you will meet with Johnny every Tuesday during fourth period, explain to Johnny that sometimes the schedule will change due to unforeseen circumstances. Not only will this help you feel better when the time comes that you *do* have to miss or reschedule a session with Johnny, but it will also provide a good opportunity to do some exploration with Johnny about change and what it feels like to him when things don't go as planned.

By communicating your schedule to staff and students, you will be allowing yourself to keep to the schedule. If there is a teacher who, despite having your schedule, still comes to speak with you when you are in session, remind them of your "free" time and tell them to come back then. It is often perceived that social workers are available at all times of the day, but this is not true. You would never go to talk to a teacher in the middle of their class lesson; you would meet with them during their free period or prep time. Teachers should do the same with you.

Communicating your schedule to teachers and staff will provide you with an excellent opportunity to talk about your role as a school social worker. The schedule lets teachers know what it is that you are doing. I can't tell you how many times I've heard from teachers about how nice I am and that I have "time for the kids." I was even told once that it was really nice what I did with the kids—coddle and support them. School social workers do a lot more than just "coddle and support" the students they work with. The teacher who called me a "coddler" did not in any way mean to downplay my profession—he simply did not understand what a school social worker does. Many times, we are in a position where we have to advocate for our students, and this can be misconstrued as "coddling" a student. Educate teachers on what you as a school social worker do. Offer them a copy of your schedule to further their understanding. Remember when you defined what you do as a school social worker at the beginning of this chapter? This is where you will get to explain exactly what you rehearsed previously.

TIP: A schedule is meant to help you organize your day. If you find that it is causing you more stress than you had before you had the schedule, then don't use it. These are just *suggestions* to help you define your role as a school social worker.

STEP 3: DEFINE YOUR ROLE WITHIN YOUR SCHEDULE

So, let's say that you have made a schedule, and it includes the following: individual counseling sessions, group sessions, prep time for professional development and paperwork, "free" time for crises or unforeseen circumstances, and meetings.

Although the schedule helps organize your day, you need to define your role within all the duties listed on it. Let's start with counseling sessions. If you are lucky, your school has a referral process in place. Perhaps you get referrals because counseling is mandated on a student's IEP. Maybe you get referrals from your supervisor. In many cases, social workers will receive referrals from all school staff, and there won't be a process in place to limit the referrals. If you are in a high school of 800 students and you are the only social worker, how do you manage your referrals? If you are like most social workers, you are eager to help *everyone* and take on as many referrals as possible. However, what you may not realize until it's too late is that you are overwhelming yourself.

STEP 4: DEFINE THE REFERRAL PROCESS

To create and sustain an effective referral process, you must state it clearly and make it easy to understand from the beginning. It is imperative that you follow the referral process to a T. If you bend the rules or accept a referral without going through the entire process you created from the start, the process will fall apart, and you will find yourself right back where you started—overwhelmed and with too many referrals.

I am going to offer you some advice on how to create an effective referral program for your school. This is meant for the general population. If students are mandated to receive counseling services on their IEP, the referral process will be different, and usually your school will have one in place. The referral process outlined here is to help those with an overwhelming amount of referrals from the general population. This is meant for the lone social worker in a school of 800 students.

Decide who is appropriate to receive social work services. Of course, everyone could benefit from some form of counseling, but in a school setting, it isn't feasible to take on every referral that comes your way. A good way to limit the amount of referrals in the first place is to create a list of appropriate conditions for when students should be referred for social work services. Here is an example list:

Conditions for referring a student for social work services:

- Severe behavior problem (define *severe* for teachers and staff—their definition may differ from yours)
- Failing two or more subjects
- Short-term crisis—loss of loved one, parents getting divorced, recent trauma, breakup with boyfriend or girlfriend, and so on
- Substance use/abuse
- Bullying
- Parent referral
- Student referral
- Mandated for services through IEP

After you have defined the conditions for referral of a student to social work services, you need to create a referral form. A referral form is not only a good way of tracking referrals for required documentation, it also cuts down on the time that a teacher or administrator will spend talking to you about a student. Before I had a referral form, I spent half my day talking to teachers about students who could benefit from my services. By the time I got the list of students, the school day was over.

Include the conditions for referring a student for services on the form. This can be a face sheet on each referral form so that the teacher or staff member knows exactly what the referral protocol is. You may also want to state some guidelines for counseling services on the referral form, such as no students are allowed to go to the social worker's office without a pass. No student should be allowed to just "drop in" to counseling—they should be *required* to be picked up from class by the social worker. Check your school's policy regarding this type of protocol. Social workers may only be allowed to see students during their free or elective periods. This should be stated on the face sheet of the referral form. You will also want to make a form that holds the referring party responsible. For example, if a teacher is referring a student for severe behavior problems in class, the teacher should be able to report the strategies and interventions they have already tried with the student. Referral to the school social worker should be a last resort, *not* the first resort. There are just too many students out there in need of social work services, and it is important to prioritize.

In addition to the part of the form that the teacher or staff member fills out, there should be a part that you fill out. This is where you will determine if the referral is appropriate for social work services or if another intervention is needed, such as referral for special education testing, more teacher interventions, a behavior intervention plan, and so on. This part of the form will also help with documentation and tracking of all referrals. If you feel the referral is appropriate for social work services, you will need to fill out the intervention section on the form. This needs to be clearly defined as well. So you want to accept the referral, but what services will the student benefit from? Individual or group counseling? Will this be a short-term or long-term case? Because of the usual overwhelming number of referrals that a school social worker receives, time-limited counseling is recommended. Start with six to eight sessions. Sometimes a student may benefit from just one or two sessions, based on their need, and then an outside referral can be given if they feel they will benefit from additional counseling/therapy. It is important to determine what services you will provide and then fill that out on the referral form. A copy of the part of the form that you fill out will be given back to the person who made the referral so that they know what the next steps will be (see the "Counseling Referral Form" on pp. 13–14).

After creating the form, you will need to have a place for referrals to be dropped off. This should be a secure place, such as a locked box with a slit in the top or a box in the front office; alternatively, people could simply slide the form under your locked door. Just make sure the forms are secured so as to protect confidentiality.

STEP 5: COMMUNICATE THE REFERRAL PROCESS

Now that you have defined the referral process for yourself, you have to introduce it to the school.

TIP: Always meet with your administrator or supervisor before introducing the process to the rest of the school staff.

A staff meeting or professional development training would be a good place to introduce the referral process. You want all school staff to be together at the same time so they all hear what you have to say. When introducing the referral process, it is good to again state your role as a school social worker, whether it is to counsel students, assist in discipline, create programs for the school, or so on. Be clear and concise when describing the referral process. Bring enough forms for every teacher and staff member so they can follow along as you explain the form. Go over the process thoroughly by explaining the conditions for referral, the referral form itself, and the place where forms should be dropped off. Then ask if anyone has any questions or needs further clarification about the referral form or the process. You may want to further explain the reason behind the referral form. Example: "I want to ensure the most effective and time-efficient manner of helping the students, and the referral process will help me, as a social worker, meet the needs of the students effectively."

STEP 6: DEFINE "FREE TIME" FOR CRISES AND UNFORSEEN CIRCUMSTANCES

You should have included some "free time" on your schedule, in addition to your prep and lunch time. This "free time" is meant for crises and other unforeseen circumstances. This is when defining your role as a school social worker is imperative. Many school social workers struggle with the boundaries of when it is appropriate to get involved and when it is not. For example, often a school social worker is called on in any type of crisis, regardless of whether it is appropriate or not, especially when a disciplinary intervention is needed. If there is a school fight, the social worker is often called in for assistance. You may be thinking, "Well, what's wrong with that?" Sometimes it is a good idea to have the social worker called when a fight breaks out, but *not* every time. Examples are provided here:

Appropriate time for the social worker to be called on: A fight breaks out between two students, and after meeting with the principal, one student reveals that they are being bullied by the other student. The school social worker should be called on for necessary intervention but *not* to handle disciplinary intervention. The social worker should never be the person to give out suspensions or disciplinary consequences. It is very important that the social worker provide interventions in times of disciplinary actions, *not* consequences. It is easy for the social worker and the administrator to mix the boundaries and role of the social worker, which is to provide intervention, *not* consequence.

Inappropriate time for social worker to be called on: A fight breaks out between two students because one student stole the other's iPod. This is clearly a situation that warrants disciplinary action by the principal or assistant principal. This should *not* be seen as a crisis situation in which the social worker needs to be called out of their daily responsibilities to assist.

Social workers often struggle with creating boundaries between being a disciplinarian and an interventionist. In the first example, the social worker is called on to offer intervention and services to the students involved in the bullying situation. The social worker is *not* called on to assist in determining disciplinary action. I caution all social workers who participate in disciplinary interventions: Be very careful when defining your role. If you are trying to gain the trust of your students in session one minute and then handing out suspensions the next, you will lose the credibility you have with the students. Remember that your role is to help, support, and advocate for the students! I am not saying that social workers should not be involved in discipline; I just think that if they are going to be involved, the boundaries and role of the social worker need to be defined precisely. This may mean, at times, that you say no to being called on for a disciplinary intervention. The second scenario is a perfect example of when a social worker should refuse to be involved and should clearly define their role as an advocate, not a disciplinarian. This can be quite difficult, especially in a school that sees the social worker as part of the disciplinary team. To avoid being called on any time a student gets sent to the office, clearly state your role—you are an interventionist and are happy to provide interventions, but you are not a disciplinarian, and if the case is clearly one for the principal or administrator, it should be left to them.

Note: The social worker is not always called in by the administrator or principal for disciplinary interventions. More often than not, it is another school staff member who seeks out the social worker first before even referring the student to the principal. An example of this would be when a hall monitor comes to your office because a student is refusing to go to class. This is a referral meant for the principal. You may think that you can help that student get back to class because you have a rapport with them, and this may be true, but then you are no longer using your time wisely or sticking to your schedule. Do *your* job, not everyone's. You can always discuss what happened with the student during your regular counseling session. In this case, redirect the hall monitor to the principal or assistant principal for appropriate disciplinary intervention.

STEP 7: CREATE YOUR JOB DESCRIPTION

No matter what position you were hired to do, defining your role is important. A tool that can help define your role as a social worker in *your* school could be developing a job description (see the "School Social Worker Position" on pp. 15–16). Sure, you may have seen the job description that was created for your position specifically, but if your school is like most others, the job description is concise and very general. Even if the school's job description is accurate to your role, it most likely does not cover *everything* that you do. Creating a job description for yourself will help you define your role as a social worker and, therefore, help you to better serve the population you work with.

SOCIAL WORKER REFERRAL PROTOCOL

Referrals: Teacher, Administrator, Student, Parent

Reason for referral:

(Please check the appropriate box)

- ❏ Severe behavior problem
- ❏ Failing two or more subjects
- ❏ Short-term crisis—loss of loved one, parents getting divorced, etc.
- ❏ Substance use/abuse
- ❏ Bullying
- ❏ Parent referral
- ❏ Student referral
- ❏ Mandated for services through IEP
     (Must fill out counselor checklist referral)

NO drop-ins. NO student comes to social worker's office without a pass. Social worker ALWAYS gets student from class. In emergency, administrator or social worker is notified. Students NEED to be in class, so counseling time will be limited and set by social worker.

**Teachers should ALWAYS take the first initial step to rectifying the problem before a referral is made to the social worker.

** If a teacher needs help or feedback before proceeding, please come and ask the social worker for assistance.

COUNSELING REFERRAL FORM

After filling out this form, please put in drop box located in the Guidance Office.

Person filling out referral form _____ Date/Time _____

Student being referred _____ Student grade _____

Advisory/Home Room teacher of student being referred _____

Reason for Referral:
(Please check the appropriate box and add specifics in the comments section)

❏ Severe behavior problem
❏ Failing two or more subjects
❏ Short-term crisis—loss of loved one, parents getting divorced, etc.
❏ Substance use/abuse
❏ Bullying
❏ Parent referral
❏ Student referral
❏ Mandated for services through IEP

Additional Comments: _____

_____

Teacher/Staff Intervention:
(Please check the box of any/all that you have done)

❏ Met with student one-on-one to correct behavior
❏ Met with student's Advisory/Home Room teacher about situation
❏ Met with student's parent/guardian   Date of meeting _____
❏ Referred student to administrator
❏ Spoken with school social worker regarding situation
❏ Tried different teaching methods to offer support for student's situation/behavior

Please Elaborate: _____

_____

Additional Comments: _____

_____

COUNSELING REFERRAL FORM (CONTINUED)

PLEASE DO NOT WRITE BELOW: SOCIAL WORKER MUST FILL OUT

Social Worker Intervention:

❏ Met with teacher/advisor/administrator
❏ Met with parent
❏ Met with student to conduct initial evaluation

_____
_____
_____
_____
_____
_____
_____
_____

Student Eligible for Counseling?   ❏ Y   ❏ N

Assigned intervention: (Circle)

Boys' Group   IEP Boys' Group   Anger Management Group

Girls' Group   IEP Girls' Group   Conflict Resolution Group

Individual Counseling:

• 6–8 sessions
• Crisis intervention counseling
• Behavior/academic intervention plan

School Social Worker Signature _____

SCHOOL SOCIAL WORKER POSITION

The primary role and purpose of this position is to design and facilitate a guidance and counseling program that ensures the academic success and emotional growth of our students. The candidate will be required to assist administrators in the development and implementation of new counseling programs, assist in student interventions, train teachers, and serve as a member of the Guidance Center team.

Some of the school social worker's responsibilities are the following:

- Counsel students, individually and in groups, regarding academic readiness, discipline, social and emotional development, substance abuse, conflict mediation, and graduation requirements and making appropriate referrals to outside agencies. Provide crisis interventions and mediations between students.

- Communicate with and in-service teachers and administrators on effective behavior management practices in the classroom as well as other professional development areas of need.

- Maintain regular and open communication with parents, including assistance in creating regular forums for parents and guardians to explore issues important to the community.

- Work closely with the Special Education Department to ensure the coordination of services for students with special needs.

- Coordinate and participate in the School Code of Conduct Committee and offer clinical expertise in regards to disciplinary interventions to teachers and administrators.

- Follow state guidelines for reporting incidents of child abuse.

- Abide by all school regulations and state requirements regarding confidentiality and education laws.

- Maintain student files, including progress notes, treatment plans, assessments, behavior contracts, and so on.

- Attend and participate in all staff and administrator meetings and trainings.

SCHOOL SOCIAL WORKER POSITION (CONTINUED)

Candidate must have a background in counseling/social work and demonstrate knowledge and skills in developing and implementing new programs in the areas of behavior management, disciplinary intervention, and multicultural and diversity issues.

Experience working with children and adolescents in a school setting strongly desired.

Bachelor's degree—Must have received your bachelor's degree from an accredited college or university in social work, counseling, psychology, or related field.

Master's degree—Must have received your master's degree from an accredited college or university in social work, counseling, psychology, or related field and be certified or licensed appropriately to work as a school social worker in the state where the position is located.

Chapter 2

INDIVIDUAL COUNSELING ACTIVITIES

This chapter includes activities and tools for the school social worker to use when conducting individual counseling sessions. Some of the activities can also be used in a group setting, but for the purpose of not repeating myself, they are listed in this chapter only. Activities and exercises in this chapter include a homework checklist, a behavior contract, exercises to be used during the engagement phase of counseling to help you get to know a student better, a simple cognitive–behavioral therapy chart, a "no harm contract" to be used as a counseling tool with at-risk students, and some relaxation exercises. It has been my experience that children, especially adolescents, have difficulty opening up when they first come to counseling with the school social worker. These exercises provide you with tools to help guide your communication and begin the counseling process. They also serve as excellent information-gathering tools for work with students you may not know well. Examples of how to use the forms are included.

The "Introduction Exercise" is meant to engage a student in conversation. It is best used during the first few sessions. This exercise can be conducted verbally as well, with the school social worker asking the student to answer the questions and the student answering them without writing them down. Either way, the exercise should incorporate the school social worker—in other words, the school social worker should ask the questions of the student, and the student should then answer them verbally or in writing. Discussion should follow each question.

Note: The exercise should not just be handed to the student to fill out. It is meant to engage the student in conversation, and therefore the social worker should ask the student the questions.

INTRODUCTION EXERCISE

Please write down or describe the following:

1. A time you felt scared:

2. A time you felt sad:

3. A time you felt happy:

4. A time you felt angry:

5. A time you felt proud of yourself:

6. A time you felt you had no control:

7. Something you are afraid of:

8. What you think/feel when you think about yourself:

9. What you think/feel when you think about your mom:

10. What you think/feel when you think about your dad:

11. What you think/feel when you think about your friends:

12. What you would describe school as:

13. Something you wish you could do over again:

14. What would you do with a million dollars?

15. Three things you like about yourself:

16. Three things you wish you could change or don't like about yourself:

17. Three things you would like to do before you die:

18. Something you would like to change in your life:

19. What is a strength that you have? When was a time you were able to use this strength to change a negative situation into a positive one?

20. How you felt while doing this exercise:

INTRODUCTION EXERCISES

I like to _____

I'm good at _____

My friends say _____ about me.

I worry when _____

One word that describes me is _____

I get angry when _____

My family is _____

I get upset when _____

I become sad when _____

I am afraid of _____

I wish _____

When I grow up I want to be _____

In ten years from now I want _____

My favorite thing to do is _____

I love _____

I hate _____

I once had a dream about _____

The "Introduction Exercises" worksheet is another tool that can be used during the engagement phase of counseling and should be used in the first or second counseling session. It is meant to engage the student in conversation.

Have the student fill out the information in silence by themselves. Afterward, discuss what the student wrote. This will begin a conversation between you and the student.

Note: It is always a good idea to check in with the student about how they are feeling while they are filling out the worksheet, especially if you see the student showing signs of emotion, such as crying, or signs of anxiety (shaking foot, biting nails, shifting in their chair). Let the student know that this is just an exercise to help you as the school social worker get to know them better, but if at any time they feel uncomfortable with any of the questions, they can stop and don't have to answer ones they don't want to.

• • •

The following "No Harm Contract" is a counseling tool and is useful when you are working with a student who has a history of cutting themselves or suicidal ideation. Having the student sign the contract forces them to promise to you and to themselves that they will not hurt themselves. Some social workers like to have a date on the contract, such as when the contract expires or when it is no longer needed.

Note: I want to be very clear when I say that this contract is *not* a substitute for a suicidality assessment. If you are with a student who is at risk of hurting themselves, you *must* take all the necessary actions to ensure that student's safety. This is covered in detail in chapter 7 ("Crisis Intervention—Protocol and Assessments"). This contract is simply a useful counseling tool for working with students who have the desire to harm themselves, either seriously or superficially.

NO HARM CONTRACT

I, _____ ,
contract and promise not to hurt myself, and if I feel the urge to hurt myself, I will do one of the following:

Tell a trusted adult, call a friend, talk to the social worker during school hours, go to a place where I am not alone, or call 911.

Signature _____

RELAXATION EXERCISES

Relaxation techniques are a great way to calm students who are overly anxious. Relaxation is also good for students who have been bullied, witnessed a trauma, or lost a loved one. Two sample relaxation techniques are provided here.

Muscle Relaxation

Before you begin this exercise, tell the student that you are going to do an exercise that will help them relax. You can ask them if they want the lights turned off. You, as the social worker, will use judgment as to whether this is appropriate or not. Sometimes turning the lights off can trigger a difficult memory or make it uncomfortable for the student or for you. Regardless of the lighting, this exercise can be performed anywhere.

Tell the student to sit comfortably in their chair with their legs uncrossed and their arms hanging at their sides. (They should not be wearing earphones or have their cell phones out.) Tell the student to close their eyes. Tell the student that you will be talking to them while their eyes are closed but that they are not to talk or answer you back.

Exercise:

"Take a deep breath in through your nose, hold it for three seconds [count to three slowly], and exhale through your mouth, slowly. Do this three times.

"Clench your toes very tightly and then release. Feel the tension releasing from your toes as you open them. Now move to your ankles and notice the tension in them. Wiggle your ankles around, releasing the tension in them. Move to your calf muscles. Tighten and release. Tighten and release. Notice the tension melting away when you release the muscle. Now move to your thigh muscles. Tense them and release. Do this slowly. Notice that you are starting to feel heavier in the chair but also lighter after releasing your tense muscles.

"Move to your stomach. Notice if there is any tension in your stomach. Take a deep breath in through your nose, hold it for three seconds [count to three slowly], and exhale through your mouth, slowly. Do this three times.

"Clench your fists. Hold for 15 seconds [count out loud to 15], then release and notice the tension melting away. Do this again.

"Shrug your shoulders and hold, then release and notice the tension melting away. Notice if you are tight in your shoulders or if it is difficult to release them.

"Move to your facial muscles. Scrunch them up and hold. Now release them and notice the tension melting away from your face. Do this two times.

"Take a deep breath in through your nose, hold it for three seconds [count to three slowly], and exhale through your mouth, slowly. Do this three more times.

"Slowly, start to open your eyes."

Guided Imagery/Creating a Safe Place

Another form of relaxation is called "guided imagery." This is the creation of a mental image that feels safe. It is delivered in a manner similar to the muscle relaxation exercise. However, guided imagery does not deal with muscle tensing and relaxing. Guided imagery is helpful for people who have panic attacks, social phobia, or test anxiety and for anyone who needs to "escape" for a moment.

Prepare the student as directed for the muscle relaxation exercise.

Before you begin this exercise, tell the student that you are going to do an exercise that will help them relax. You can ask them if they want the lights turned off. You, as the social worker, will use judgment as to whether this is appropriate or not. Sometimes turning the lights off can trigger a difficult memory or make it uncomfortable for the student or for you. Regardless of the lighting, this exercise can be performed anywhere.

Tell the student to sit comfortable in their chair with their legs uncrossed and their arms hanging at their sides. (They should not be wearing earphones or have their cell phones out.) Tell the student to close their eyes. Tell the student that you will be talking to them while their eyes are closed and asking them questions but that they are not to talk or answer you back, only to think about what you are saying.

Exercise:

"Take a deep breath in through your nose, hold it for three seconds [count to three slowly], and exhale through your mouth, slowly. Do this three times.

"I want you to imagine a place where you feel safe. Maybe it is a place you have been before. Maybe it is a place you have never visited. Perhaps you have seen this place in a dream or a movie. Picture this safe place. What do you see? Are you on a beach? Are you outside? Inside? Are you alone, or are you with someone? Who is there with you? Do you have a pet with you? Are there other animals where you are? What do you smell? What do you hear? Is it noisy in your safe place, or is it quiet?

"How do you feel in your safe place? What are you doing in your safe place? Are you awake? Are you sleeping? Are you walking? Are you running?

"What is good about your safe place? Visualize this safe place in its entirety."

HOMEWORK CHECKLIST

Class	Mon.	Tues.	Wed.	Thurs.	Fri.	Parent Initials

HOMEWORK CHECKLIST EXAMPLE

Class	Mon.	Tues.	Wed.	Thurs.	Fri.	Parent Initials
Pre-Algebra						
Global						
English						
Visual Arts						
Business						
Science						
Sports Journalism						

Ask the student to begin to come back to reality and slowly open their eyes (when they are ready). Tell the student that they can go to their safe place when they feel sad, angry, or scared. They can do this at night to help them fall asleep, or they can "escape" to their safe place for just a few seconds at a time—for example, right before taking a test in class.

Both of these relaxation exercises are extremely useful because you can do them over and over again with students. In addition, students can do them on their own. One of my students recorded me (with my permission) doing a relaxation exercise and used it to help him fall asleep at night.

• • •

The "Homework Checklist" is an excellent tool for tracking homework for a student with organization issues. Many times, an assignment pad gets lost or is deemed overwhelming by the student. A simple homework checklist is easy to use and also holds the student accountable for their homework, as there is a section that requires parent initials. I have had many parents call me up and tell me that their son or daughter never has any homework. I'm sure you have all heard this too! Although it is important to encourage the parent to speak with their child's teacher, you can also suggest a homework checklist. The checklist is really for the student to use, but it allows the parent to see what the child has for homework and sign off on it. The checklist can be monitored by the teacher, parent, social worker, or all.

Note: When introducing the checklist to the student, tell them that you are trying to help them remember their homework as well as communicate with their parents. At first, the student may be resistant. However, with the right approach and explanation, they will usually see that you are indeed trying to help them. Most often the student is sick of their parent constantly yelling at them for not knowing their assignments and desperately wants the parent to stop calling the school, which may be getting the student in trouble with their teachers. More often than not, when a student doesn't complete their homework, they are not trying to be malicious or lazy—it is because they have problems with organization or remembering. This easy-to-use checklist can help the student with these issues.

• • •

Behavior charts are extremely useful for children and young teens. They can be used at home with parents or in school. They are concrete and clear. Behavior charts are helpful for both children and parents. In the past, parents have said to me that their child

BEHAVIOR CHART

CHORE/BEHAVIOR	POINTS

POINTS—CERTAIN NUMBER OF POINTS ALLOWS CHILD/ADOLESCENT TO GET A REWARD/PRIVILEGE.

- Privileges and rewards are defined by child/adolescent AND adult before beginning point chart.

- Number of points needed to gain a privilege is discussed before beginning point chart.

BEHAVIOR CHART EXAMPLE

CHORE/BEHAVIOR	POINTS
Brush teeth	
Make bed	
Clean up toys after use	
Read for 30 minutes	
Complete homework	
Clean room—be specific	
Take out garbage	
Wash dishes	
Set table	
Show respect—be specific	
Express feelings	
Tell the truth	
Show politeness	
Receive good report/reports card from school	

POINTS—CERTAIN NUMBER OF POINTS ALLOWS CHILD/ADOLESCENT TO GET A REWARD/PRIVILEGE.

- Privileges and rewards are defined by child/adolescent AND adult before beginning point chart.

- Number of points needed to gain a privilege is discussed before beginning point chart.

doesn't do any chores. Then, when I bring this concern up with the child, they answer, "Well, I don't get anything when I do chores, so what's the point?" A behavior chart not only keeps track of the chores the child does, it also rewards the child with privileges. Behavior charts like the one provided here are easy to use and can be altered in any way. I have provided you with an example chart as well as an easy-to-use template. You can change any or all of the chores/behaviors and add different ones, or you can make it school based and replace the chores with homework or class work. You will notice that the chores/behaviors are listed on one side of the chart and points are listed on the other.

You may notice that in my example chart, I have added "be specific" in certain areas. What I mean by this is that the chore/behavior can change depending on the child and adult. For example, "show respect" is one of the behaviors that I chose for the example chart. I added "be specific" because *respect* can be defined in many different ways. Your definition of respect may be different than someone else's. So, when introducing this chart to the student and their parent(s), make sure that you define the behaviors clearly. The child *must* understand what all chores/behaviors mean, otherwise they will not be able to perform them. The number of points earned for each chore/behavior should be consistent. For example, you get one point for making your bed and another point for washing the dishes. It should not be that washing dishes is worth three points and making the bed is worth only one. This will cause the child to do only the chores that are worth the most points, and you don't want that. When introducing this chart to the student and parent(s), make sure that the point system and the number of points needed to earn a privilege are clear. If the child earns a million points but never gets rewarded, you will have an extinction burst, and the child will no longer value the chart. Tell the child's parent(s) that they *need* to be consistent. As soon as the number of points agreed upon is reached, the child should receive their reward/privilege. Some parents won't want to reward their child until the end of the week. This is fine—just make sure that this is clearly stated to and understood by the child.

• • •

The next exercise is great for middle and high school students who need to take a closer look at their behaviors. School social workers can use this simple "Cognitive–Behavioral Therapy [CBT] Exercise" even if they have not received formal CBT training. The chart basically tracks a student's thoughts and behaviors in an effort to change negative behaviors into positive ones. When using this tool with a student, make sure you explain the chart thoroughly and define what the words used mean. Tell the

COGNITIVE–BEHAVIORAL THERAPY EXERCISE FOR CHANGING THOUGHTS AND BEHAVIORS

ANTECEDENT— WHAT HAPPENED?	AUTOMATIC THOUGHT— INTERNAL DIALOGUE	BEHAVIOR RESULTING FROM AUTOMATIC THOUGHT	CONSEQUENCE OF BEHAVIOR

COGNITIVE–BEHAVIORAL THERAPY EXERCISE FOR CHANGING THOUGHTS AND BEHAVIORS EXAMPLE

ANTECEDENT— WHAT HAPPENED?	AUTOMATIC THOUGHT— INTERNAL DIALOGUE	BEHAVIOR RESULTING FROM AUTOMATIC THOUGHT	CONSEQUENCE OF BEHAVIOR
I FAILED MY TEST.	I'M STUPID.	I SHUT DOWN IN CLASS AND DIDN'T DO CLASS WORK.	I FAILED FOR THE DAY.
MY SISTER GOT MAD AT ME FOR GOING IN HER ROOM.	I'M AN IDIOT AND SHOULD HAVE KNOWN BETTER.	I WENT AND CUT MYSELF BECAUSE I FELT LONELY AND UPSET FOR MAKING MY SISTER MAD AT ME.	I WENT TO THE HOSPITAL. MOM FOUND OUT THAT I CUT AND GOT MAD AT ME.

student that you are going to do an exercise that is going to help them understand their thoughts and behaviors. Show them the CBT chart and explain how tracking thoughts and feelings will help you and them to better understand their behaviors. Tell the student that you are going to take a look at their behaviors and the thoughts and feelings they feel *before* they engage in them.

Explain the chart and define the words used on the chart:

Antecedent: Tell the student that an antecedent is what happened to make them feel a certain way that resulted in a behavior (usually negative). Example: "Another student called you a jerk and then you cursed at him and got sent to the principal's office. The 'antecedent' is the other student calling you a name."

Internal dialogue: This part is tricky. Trying to explain to a student what an internal dialogue is can be challenging. Here is an example of how you may explain it to an adolescent student: "We all talk to ourselves. Not necessarily out loud, but in our minds. I'm not saying that we hear voices [student may laugh], but we talk to ourselves. For example, I might say to myself (in my mind) tonight I have to do the laundry, make dinner, et cetera. This is called our 'internal dialogue.'"

Automatic thought: This definition is also tricky. Try explaining it by tying in the internal dialogue definition like this: "Okay, so I have explained internal dialogue to you in that we all talk to ourselves. Well, sometimes what we say to ourselves can be automatic, to the point where we may not even realize it. This is called an 'automatic thought' and is part of our internal dialogue. For example, if you make a mistake on an exam, your automatic thought may be that you think you are stupid. Your internal dialogue may even be that you say to yourself, 'I'm such an idiot.' What makes the thoughts automatic is that you don't even realize you have them. After saying these things over and over to yourself, they become automatic. Hence, they are called automatic thoughts.

"In the example I gave above about another student calling you a name and then you cursing at him, which resulted in your getting sent to the principals' office, the automatic thought or internal dialogue that may have occurred could be that you said to yourself, 'I'm gonna kill that kid.' Or, 'He's right when he called me a jerk—I am a jerk.' Automatic thoughts are automatic, so you may not even notice them. If I asked you about a recent situation where you got in trouble, you might not even be able to recall the thought that resulted in your behavior. This is where this chart is going to help us. In order to change your behaviors, you are going to need to recognize and understand your automatic thoughts first. This is the tricky part."

Behavior: Tell the student that the behavior resulting from the automatic thought or internal dialogue is what the student did in response. "In the same example we are using, your response to your automatic thought was to curse at the other student. This is the 'behavior.'"

Consequence: Tell the student that the consequence is what happened as a result of the behavior. Consequences can be either positive or negative—they are just what happened as a result of the behavior. "In the example we have been using about the student who called you a jerk, the consequence for you cursing at him was that you were sent to the principal's office."

Say to student, "By using this chart together, we are going to examine your automatic thoughts and internal dialogues to help us better understand your behaviors."

Note: The chart can be given to the student to take with them and track their automatic thoughts, behaviors, and consequences, or it can be completed with you during counseling sessions, or both. Regardless of how you to decide to use the chart, my advice is to fill out at least one full set of "Antecedent," "Automatic Thought," "Behavior," and "Consequence" sections together with the student so that they know how to do it in the future. Also, getting students to recognize their automatic thoughts can be quite a challenge. If you find that the student is having difficulty with this in the beginning, you may want to start off simply by giving them a counseling homework assignment of tracking their automatic thoughts. They can simply write down their thoughts or feelings after a situation occurs that causes them to get upset. Instruct them to write down what they said to themselves or what their automatic thought was. Give them more examples of when automatic thoughts may occur, such as when their mother or father yells at them, when they are rejected by a girl or boy for a date, when they fail a test or make a mistake, when they look in the mirror, and so on.

Note: The CBT tool is excellent for tracking thoughts in an effort to change negative behaviors to positives ones, but it can also be used to change negative thought patterns. For example, a teen who is struggling with the beginning stages of an eating disorder may not be engaging in the negative behaviors yet, but the distorted thinking patterns *can* be present. So if a student's automatic thought is "I'm so fat," this can be tracked and challenged as well.

• • •

I have had great success with the next tool because it is concrete and easy for students to understand. It is also an eye-opening and powerful tool for counseling sessions as it forces students to take a closer look at their thoughts and behaviors.

Behavior contracts are useful tools for students who are struggling with behavior problems. Behavior contracts should be concrete, concise, and easy to understand

BEHAVIOR CONTRACT

Student Name: _____ Date: _____

Homeroom Teacher: _____ Grade: _____

These are my commitments/goals:

1. _____

2. _____

3. _____

These are the rewards/privileges I will receive if I meet my goals:

1. _____

2. _____

3. _____

These are the consequences that will occur if I don't meet my goals:

1. _____

2. _____

3. _____

My contract will be reviewed on: _____

I _____ agree to this contract and
　　　　　　　　　　　　　[Student Name]
understand that I will receive rewards and consequences for my actions and behaviors.

Signatures:

Student: _____ Parent: _____

Social Worker: _____ Principal: _____

Other: _____

BEHAVIOR CONTRACT EXAMPLE

Student Name: _John Smith_____ Date: _3/25/2011_____

Homeroom Teacher: _Ms. Hebert_____ Grade: _8_____

These are my commitments/goals:

1. _To complete all work in all my classes every day_____

2. _To raise my hand when I have a question or answer_____

3. _To ask for help when I don't understand the assignment_____

These are the rewards/privileges I will receive if I meet my goals:

1. _Positive phone call to parents_____

2. _10 min. free time (reading, drawing, computer time)_____

3. _Pack of playing cards or special pen_____

These are the consequences that will occur if I don't meet my goals:

1. _Lunch detention_____

2. _No free time for the class period_____

3. _Phone call home to parent_____

My contract will be reviewed on: _____

I _____ agree to this contract and
                              [Student Name]
understand that I will receive rewards and consequences for my actions and behaviors.

Signatures:

Student: _____   Parent: _____

Social Worker: _____   Principal: _____

Other: _____

for all involved. They are easy to use and hold everyone involved accountable—most important, the student. The behavior contract shown here has the student making commitments and setting goals about their behavior and, in return, receiving rewards/privileges or consequences.

Note: Students requiring a behavior contract should be involved in creating the commitments/goals. A behavior contract won't work if the teacher, social worker, or administrator forces the student to agree to commitments/goals that they have not been involved in creating. Think about it: Would you yourself commit to something you had no say in? This also applies to the rewards/privileges and consequences. If the student doesn't care about the rewards listed on the contract, they are unlikely to change their behavior. Of course, students need to follow rules and must abide by the rules of their school regardless of how they feel about them, but in my experience, a behavior contract will be much more successful if the student is involved in creating it.

Behavior contracts can be altered and changed at any time. They should also be reviewed periodically and, at those times, changed or destroyed altogether. Hopefully, a time will come when the student no longer requires the behavior contract.

Chapter 3

GROUP IMPLEMENTATION AND COUNSELING ACTIVITIES

This chapter includes activities and tools used when creating and implementing group counseling sessions, including how to begin a group from the ground up. Activities in this section include an anger management group; body image and love and healthy relationship activities for adolescent girls; diversity, prejudice, and letter-writing exercises; and exercises that deal with bullying prevention and social skill building.

Groups can be difficult to begin in schools. Issues such as scheduling, selecting participants, finding appropriate space, and marketing can cause major difficulties when implementing a group.

GETTING SUPPORT

When starting a group in a school setting, you will need the support of your administrators and teachers. Start off by sharing your idea with your principal or assistant principal. If they are on board, then go to the next level, which is to get the teachers on board.

TIP: Ask for teachers' feedback. When would they prefer you to run the group? You won't get the teachers on board if you plan to run your group during essential class time, such as English or math. For example, if you know that Mr. Smith gives a quiz every Friday during third period, running a group Friday third period is probably not the best idea. Obviously, because of scheduling conflicts and the short amount of time in a school day, you won't be able to make everyone happy. I'm just saying that you should try to minimize scheduling conflicts as much as possible. Try offering the group during student lunch, gym, or elective classes.

MARKETING YOUR GROUP

You have this great idea to start a group, but you have no participants. So you have to market your idea. You can do this by word of mouth—telling some of the students you see for counseling, sharing it with teachers, and announcing it at staff meetings and over the PA system. You can also make flyers to post around the school. After you get interest in your group, you need to select your participants. You don't just start a group by getting referrals or interest in the group. *Not* everyone is suitable for the group setting. I strongly urge you to interview potential participants. It is important to keep the group small. On average, eight to 10 students is ideal, but groups that are larger or smaller can still be successful. If you have too many appropriate participants, create more than one group. Use your judgment in determining the appropriate size for the group.

INTERVIEWING PARTICIPANTS

Some questions to help guide you through the interview process are provided here:

- "Have you even been in a group before?"
- "What do you think you will gain from being part of this group? What do you want to gain or learn?"
- "What is the reason you want to be part of this group?"
- "Can you commit to coming to group each week?"
- "Will you be able to be honest and open in group?"
- "How do you usually handle conflict?"
- "If someone says something in group that you disagree with, how will you react?"
- "Do you understand what confidentiality is? Will you be able to uphold the confidentiality rule in group?"

Okay, so you have your administrators and teachers on board, you have identified your group participants, and the schedule is set. All you need now is a space for the group. In an ideal world, you would have a beautiful, spacious office where the group can take place. But if you are like most school social workers, your space is an office converted from a storage closet. Finding an appropriate space can be tricky. You may have to do some research. Maybe a classroom is available during the time you want to run your group. Maybe there is another office that you can use for one period a week. Perhaps there is a conference room available for use to run your group. When attempting to find space for your group, enlist the help of your administrators. If they support your group, they will help you find space.

FIRST GROUP SESSION

How you are perceived during the first session of the group is critical to how the group will run. This is the time to let the group know that you are the facilitator but you are also *in charge*. You, and only you, have the right to interrupt group members. The first session is the one in which group rules need to be created and discussed. Allow the group to come up with its own rules. Keep these rules visible at each group session. Hang them on the wall so that group members are reminded of them each week. If a participant breaks a rule, you can easily guide them back to the rules by pointing to where they are posted. Some sample rules are listed on the next page.

TIP: If the group has trouble allowing everyone to talk without interrupting, you can use an object such as a ball or a stick and call it the "Talking Ball" or "Talking Stick." The rule is that the only person who can talk is the one who has the Talking Ball or the Talking Stick. Group members then pass the ball or stick to other members when it is their turn to speak.

Through my years as a school social worker, I have led many different groups. Some were for middle or high school students, and others were for elementary students. Some dealt with sensitive issues such as body image, relationships, anger management, bullying, prejudice, and racism. Others dealt with less sensitive topics such as social skills, identifying your strengths, substance abuse, and behavior management. These groups and how to effectively lead them are the subject of this chapter.

ANGER MANAGEMENT GROUP

Materials: Floppy binders or folders for all group participants, pens, pencils, dry erase/chalk board or pad on easel

Time: Seven weeks, 45-minute sessions

This is a very structured, seven-week group. It is also a *closed* group, which means that all participants will start at week 1 of the group and finish at week 7. No new participants will be added in the middle of the group. This group is a voluntary group. In my

GROUP RULES

CONFIDENTIALITY—What is said here, stays here.

RESPECT EACH OTHER

KEEP HANDS TO SELF

CLEAN UP—Push chairs in and clean up group room at the end of group.

ONE PERSON SPEAKS AT A TIME—No interrupting!

HAVE FUN!!

experience, anger management groups do *not* work as well if they are mandated. Students have to want to come to the group and participate. This will yield the best results. The group should be kept small and be gender specific. In other words, there should not be a mixed group with female and male students. In my experience, this group works better when it is just female students or just male students. Although you may receive referrals from teachers and administrators for this group, you should use your discretion as to whom you choose to put in the group. The group should be kept to a maximum of 10 participants. Also, interviewing potential participants is essential. Some students may benefit from anger management, but not all students are appropriate for a group setting. Conducting short interviews with potential participants is helpful in selecting the appropriate ones. In the event that there are more than 10 appropriate participants, run more than one group. Because the group only runs for seven weeks, you can start another section of the group after the first one finishes. However, to get the most effective results, I urge you to *not* include more than 10 participants.

You will need certain materials for this group, such as a large area for you to write on; that can be a dry erase board, a chalk board, or a large pad on an easel. You will also need pens and pencils as well as binders or folders for every member of the group. (You will not use the binders/folders until the second group session.) Other materials will include copies of worksheets. Each session section explains exactly what you will need for that particular session.

Each session of the seven group sessions is described step by step, including what to do and how to effectively lead the session.

Week 1

Establishing Group Comfort

- The group should be small in size (10 students or fewer).
- The group will meet once a week for 45 minutes.
- The group will be a closed group. This means that all participants will attend all seven sessions, and no new admissions will be made to the group while it is running.

Introduce yourself as the group leader and explain the purpose of the group to the participant (five minutes).

Purpose: "This group is meant for students who feel that they have issues dealing with their anger and behavior and would like to learn different ways of dealing with them. This group will provide you with coping mechanisms as well as positive replacement behaviors for handling anger effectively. This group will be a teaching group. Although you will be allowed and asked to share your thoughts and opinions, this group is not meant to be an open forum. You will be *taught* in this group."

Explain to the group that this group will run for seven and only seven weeks, that the sessions will be filled with activities and lessons, and that participation is required. Express to the group that this is a short anger management group, that it is only an introduction, and that it will touch briefly on anger management issues. After the group is over, if there are participants that feel they need more intensive anger management, let them know that they can come to you privately for more services or for a referral to other appropriate services.

Explain Confidentiality and When It Needs to Be Broken (Five Minutes)

Confidentiality: "Nothing that is said in this room will be shared with anyone outside of this group. We should all agree to this. This means that no student talks about what is said in here with their friends or girlfriend or boyfriend if they are not in this group. The only times that confidentiality will be broken are as follows:

"*suicide*—if someone reveals that they want to hurt themselves;

"*homicide*—if someone reveals that they want to hurt someone else;

"*child abuse*—if someone reveals that they are being abused; and

"*substance abuse*—if someone comes to the group under the influence of drugs or alcohol."

Go around to each participant and ask if they can agree to the confidentiality agreement. Do not continue the group until everyone nods in agreement.

Group Member Introductions (10 to 15 Minutes)

Next, go around to each of the group members and ask them to introduce themselves. Ask each member to share their name, their age, and why they feel they should be a part of this group. They can elaborate on ways they would like to change their anger or not. Feel out the comfort level. Encourage everyone to share, but tell the group that if anyone is uncomfortable talking today, it is okay to pass.

Group Rules (10 Minutes)

After each member introduces themselves, tell the group that you need to establish rules or guidelines for the group. Group rules were discussed previously in this section. Remember that the group members should be the ones to come up with the rules. You can add or alter rules when necessary.

Give an example of a group rule, such as "respect each other" or "one person talks at a time." You will write down all rules the group comes up with and display them each time the group meets.

Wrap-up (Five Minutes)

Keep the wrap-up consistent every week. Do this at the end of every group session. You may encounter resistance initially from group participants, but it is essential that you tell the group that at times sensitive issues will arise during group, and it is important for them to relax and compose themselves again before leaving group. Remember that after the students leave the group, they have to go back to class or to lunch—they do not have the luxury of going home, as they would if they were leaving a therapy session at a clinic. It is your job to make sure that the group members are able to go back to class after dealing with some heavy issues while in group.

Tell the group that you are going to do a relaxation exercise. Turn off the lights and ask for complete silence. Tell the group members to close their eyes and take a slow deep breath in through their nose and hold it for five seconds (count out loud to five), and then tell them to release it through their mouth. Tell the group to release tension each time they exhale.

Repeat this three times. Turn on the lights and ask the group how they are feeling. Dismiss the group and tell them you will see them next week at the same time. Remind them of the commitment they made to come every week to group for the entire seven weeks.

Week 2

Check-in (Five Minutes)

Before getting into this week's content, you should check in with the students to see how they are doing. You do not have to ask each student individually; it should just be a general check-in: "How's everyone doing? How has this week been so far? How was your weekend? Did anyone have any questions or reactions to last week's group?"

This part should run smoothly and quickly. It's just a quick introduction, yet it makes the group participants come together and feel comfortable with one other.

Hand Out Binders/Folders (Five Minutes)

Explain to the group that these folders are for them. Throughout the group, the members will be receiving worksheets and other materials that they will need to keep in a collection for use after the group is over. You will collect the folders at the end of each session, and the group members will get to keep the folders only after the full seven weeks is over. Explain to the group that the reason for this is that between group sessions, you will be adding things to their folders.

Introduce the Lesson for the Day: Triggers, Cues, and Behaviors

Tell the group that today's lesson is about the breakdown of anger into three categories. Make a chart on the board as shown here:

TRIGGERS	CUES	BEHAVIORS

Define triggers (five minutes): "*Triggers*: Things in the environment that make you angry. Think of a trigger on a gun. If you pull it, the gun goes off. Triggers are things that 'set you off.' Examples are lying, stealing, getting a bad grade, your parents, or a recent argument with a friend or girlfriend or boyfriend."

Go around to each member of the group and ask them to share some of their "triggers." Make a list of the group's triggers in the chart on the board.

Define cues (seven minutes): "*Cues*: The physical, emotional, and body sensations one feels when one is angry. Cues are physiological occurrences in the body. Examples are sweating, racing heart, tearing, gritting teeth, clenching fist, flaring nostrils, or face turning red."

Go around to each member of the group and ask them to share some of their anger "cues." The group may have trouble understanding this and may mix cues up with triggers or what makes them angry. Remind them that cues are things happening to their bodies, usually without them knowing it. Add the group's cues list to the chart.

Define behaviors (five minutes): "*Behaviors*: These are what you do when you are angry. They are how one reacts when one is feeling angry or enraged. Examples include punching a locker, yelling, screaming into a pillow, shutting down, or getting into a fist fight."

Again, go around and ask each member what they do when they are angry. Add the group's behaviors to the chart.

You should have a comprehensive chart now. Tell the group that you are going to only focus on the "Behaviors" column for now (eight minutes).

Ask the group which behaviors are 100 percent effective—in other words, they work all the time. If a behavior only works sometimes, it gets crossed off the list. A behavior is *only* effective if it works *every* time! For example, if a student says that fighting is effective, challenge the student with the fact that there is a chance they could get hurt in a fight or suspended from school. This means the behavior is *not* always effective. It would then get crossed off the list. Point this out to the group.

Recap and ask the group to define the three categories of anger: (1) triggers, (2) cues, and (3) behaviors (five minutes).

Hand out the "Triggers, Cues, Behaviors Worksheet (see p. 46) (10 minutes).

Ask the group to fill it out individually. Tell them that you just talked about the group's triggers, cues, and behaviors but now want them to focus specifically on *their own* triggers, cues, and behaviors. Tell them that this is for their knowledge only and to help them recognize how the three categories of anger manifest in each of them. This will go in their folders and will not be shared with the group.

Wrap-up (Five Minutes)

Tell the group that you are going to do a relaxation exercise. Turn off the lights and ask for complete silence. Tell the group members to close their eyes and take a slow deep breath in through their nose and hold it for five seconds (count out loud to five), and then tell them to release it through their mouth. Tell the group to release tension each time they exhale.

Repeat this three times. Turn on the lights and ask the group how they are feeling.

Hand out the "What Leads to Anger? worksheet (see p. 47). Tell the group that this is not homework but that they should add it to their binder for when the group is over, as a tool to help them identify their triggers.

Dismiss the group and tell them you will see them next week at the same time. Remind them of the commitment they made to come every week to group for the entire seven weeks.

Note: Before next group, you should type up the comprehensive list of triggers,

TRIGGERS, CUES, BEHAVIORS WORKSHEET

Fill this out according to YOUR triggers, cues, and behaviors. This is for YOU and will not be shared with the group.

TRIGGERS (What sets me off like a trigger on a gun?)	CUES (What happens inside my body when I get angry?)	BEHAVIORS (How do I react when I become angry? What do I do?)

WHAT LEADS TO ANGER?

Sometimes people become angry when they feel sad, ignored, embarrassed, or frustrated.

What makes you feel sad? _____

_____

_____

_____

What makes you feel ignored?_____

_____

_____

_____

What makes you feel embarrassed?_____

_____

_____

_____

What makes you feel frustrated? _____

_____

_____

_____

Do any of your answers match your "anger triggers"? Which ones: _____

_____

_____

_____

cues, and behaviors. *Important:* The list should include *all* behaviors, even the ones that were crossed off due to not being 100 percent effective. The reason to include these behaviors is to show the group members how they are managing their behaviors currently. They are in the anger management group because they want to learn *new* behaviors. If you want, you can include the ineffective behaviors in a separate section of the list titled "Ineffective Behaviors," or you can just leave them on the list crossed out or with a check mark over them. This is to point out to the group that they have been handling their anger in some inappropriate ways up to this point.

Make enough copies for the entire group, and add it to their folders for future use.

Week 3

Check-in (Five Minutes)

Before getting into this week's content, you should check in with the students to see how they are doing. You do not have to ask each student individually; it should just be a general check-in: "How's everyone doing? How has this week been so far? How was your weekend? Did anyone have any questions or reactions to last week's group?"

This part should run smoothly and quickly. It's just a quick introduction, yet it makes the group come together and feel comfortable with each other.

Hand out binders/folders to each group member.

Review of Last Group Session (Five Minutes)

Quickly review the content from last week's group. Ask the group to define the three categories of anger: (1) cues, (2) triggers, and (3) behaviors. Help them if they forgot the definitions or mix the categories up.

Group Share (25 Minutes)

This meeting will run more like an open therapy group, but you will still be the facilitator. You will ask each member to take a moment to think about the last time they became really angry. If they are having trouble coming up with the last time they became angry, tell them they can use any time they can think of.

Go around to each of the students and ask them the following: "Tell me about the last time you became very angry. What happened to make you so angry? What was going on inside your body when you became angry? What did you feel? What did you do? How did you react?"

After each person shares their anger story, ask the group to identify the triggers, cues, and behaviors for each person. Example: Johnny tells a story about how he became very angry when his sister borrowed his iPod without asking and lost it. Johnny noticed that he was sweating and turning red when he became angry. Johnny said he became so angry that he ended up punching his little sister in the stomach and got grounded by his mother.

After Johnny's story, you would then turn to the group and ask, "What were Johnny's triggers, cues, and behaviors?" Sometimes the cues won't be as obvious as they are in Johnny's story. If this is the case, you can turn back to Johnny and ask him if he remembers what was happening inside his body when he became angry (these are the cues).

Wrap-up (Five Minutes)

Tell the group that you are going to do a relaxation exercise. Turn off the lights and ask for complete silence. Tell the group members to close their eyes and take a slow deep breath in through their nose and hold it for five seconds (count out loud to five), and then tell them to release it out through their mouth. Tell the group to release tension each time they exhale. Repeat this three times. Turn on the lights and ask the group how they are feeling.

TIP: This week may have made some of the group members angry because you asked them to recall a time when they became very angry. Make sure that all group members are calm enough to return to class. If this is not the case after the wrap-up, do another few deep breaths with the group and then dismiss them.

Week 4

Check-in (Five Minutes)

Before getting into this week's content, you should check in with the students to see how they are doing. You do not have to ask each student individually; it should just be a general check-in: "How's everyone doing? How has this week been so far? How was your weekend? Did anyone have any questions or reactions to last week's group?"

This part should run smoothly and quickly. It's just a quick introduction, yet it makes the group come together and feel comfortable with each other.

Hand out binders/folders to each group member.

Group Share (10 Minutes)

Ask the group if anyone had an anger outburst or a situation in which they became angry over the past week. Ask for volunteers to share their story. Limit the sharing to one or two people so that you don't lose track of time.

After the participants share, ask the group for feedback with some guiding questions: "How do you think _____ handled the situation? What could he [or she] have done differently? What were his [or her] triggers, cues, and behaviors?" (Yes, you are drilling these words into the minds of the group participants!) "How would you have handled the situation if you were faced with what _____ was faced with?"

Lesson (Five to 10 Minutes)

Introduce the lesson for the day: coping mechanisms.

Say to the group, "Now you have figured out and discussed your anger cues, triggers, and behaviors and why you become angry. We have discussed what each of you do when you become angry and how you handle it. We have seen that many of your behaviors have proven to be ineffective. [Remind the group about the not 100 percent effective exercise.] Now we have to figure out how to handle anger in a positive and effective manner." Define *coping mechanisms*.

"*Coping mechanisms*: skills and ways of handling anger in a positive and effective manner."

Ask the group to open their binders/folders and look at the "Behaviors" list again. (This is part of the three-column list created in week 2, which you typed up and placed in their binders/folders.)

Go around to each member and ask in what ways they would like to change their behaviors or how they handle anger (10 to 15 minutes).

They should all want to change at least one thing about their behaviors. Do *not* accept answers like "I don't want to change anything." If you get an answer like this, respond with this: "Was there ever a time in your life that you were angry and felt that you didn't handle your anger as you wanted to? Perhaps there was a time that you could not control your anger the way you wanted to and ended up doing something you regretted." This should give the student some ideas of what they want to change.

Wrap-up (Five Minutes)

Tell the group that you are going to do a relaxation exercise. Turn off the lights and ask for complete silence. Tell the group members to close their eyes and take a slow deep breath in through their nose and hold it for five seconds (count out loud to five), and then tell them to release it out through their mouth. Tell the group to release tension each time they exhale. Repeat this three times. Turn on the lights and ask the group how they are feeling.

Dismiss the group and tell them you will see them next week at the same time. Remind them of the commitment they made to come every week to group for the entire seven weeks.

Week 5

Check-in (Five Minutes)

Before getting into this week's content, you should check in with the students to see how they are doing. You do not have to ask each student individually; it should just be a general check in. "How's everyone doing? How has this week been so far? How was your weekend? Did anyone have any questions or reactions to last week's group?"

This part should run smoothly and quickly. It's just a quick introduction, yet it makes the group come together and feel comfortable with each other.

Hand out binders/folders to each group member.

Contract (10 Minutes)

A bit about the contract (see p. 57): This group session can be altered to fit the needs of your school. The contract part of the session is meant for small schools that can put supports in place for when students need a "break" or "time out." It is meant for students with severe emotional disturbances or who get "out of control." To implement the contract, the school's administrator, principal, teacher, and social worker need to all be on board. In *no way* am I suggesting you implement the contract part of this group without speaking to your administrator or principal first. If, after reviewing the contract piece of this group, you do not believe it will be feasible to implement it at you school, simply skip the contract portion of this group and continue on to the "Coping Mechanisms" section.

For those interested in using the contract, it is explained here.

Hand out the "Anger Management Contract" to each of the group members.

Instruct them to fill out the contract, writing down three "Safe Places" and three "Safe People" they can go to when they are angry. Tell the group that this is a contract for use in the school and that the "Safe Places" and "Safe People" are places and people they have access to while in school. Examples of "Safe Places" are the guidance office, the main office, the lunch room, hallways (when the student has a pass), and so on. Examples of "Safe People" are the social worker or counselor, a hall monitor, a teacher, the principal, a friend, and so on. Limit the number of friends that students write down to only one. Explain to them that the reason for this is that they may not be able to access a friend at certain times, because their friends may be in class when they become angry.

Note: The reason friends are allowed as "Safe People" at all is that some students don't feel comfortable talking with adults when they are angry. Some students also have that one person who can calm them down when they are angry, such as a boyfriend, girlfriend, or best friend.

Remember: Prior to giving the contract to the students to fill out, you should have already spoken with the principal and teachers regarding the process of implementing the contract. The worst thing a social worker could do is introduce an anger management technique like the contract and have it not upheld.

Explain to the group that the contract is a *privilege* and is *not* a free pass out of class or something to be taken advantage of. The contract is to be used when and *only* when a group member feels that they are getting out of control and very angry and cannot remain in the class because of the escalation of their anger. The student is to present the contract to the teacher (as they will have a copy on them at all times). The teacher will then (at their discretion) allow the student to go to one of their "Safe Places" or see one of their "Safe People."

Note: A time limit should be decided on and possibly included in the contract. Example: The student is allowed to go to their "Safe Place" for a duration of five minutes. This way, the student is not missing the entire class period. However, use judgment when creating the time limit; depending on how angry a student is, they may need more time in their "Safe Place" or with their "Safe Person." Sometimes a student is so angry that returning to class is not an option. Get your administrator involved if this is the case.

Note: The contract is meant as a tool to prevent the student from becoming "out of control" or the need for disciplinary action or therapeutic holds (in a case in which restraint is necessary). It has been my experience that many schools are *very* reactive when problems occur, and the contract is meant to be proactive in the effort to prevent unnecessary reactions from school administration and other personnel.

After each student fills out the contract, instruct them to sign it at the bottom where it says "Student Signature."

You will collect the contracts and sign each one where it says "Social Worker/ Counselor Signature." After the group session is over, you will get the signatures of the administrator or principal and teachers.

TIP: If a student in the anger management group is classified and receiving special education services, it may be beneficial to include the contract in the student's IEP or behavior intervention plan. This will ensure the implementation of the contract by all school staff.

I know you are probably thinking that there is no way that the contract will work or that you will get the teachers on board. It *does* work! I have used this contract in two schools, and it works! There will be certain times when a student tries to take advantage of the contract and use it as a free pass to get out of class, but on average that won't happen. If it does, it is best to speak with that student and explain the whole reason the contract was created to begin with—as an anger management coping mechanism. Remind the student that it is a privilege and that if they are unable to be mature and responsible enough to use it appropriately, they will lose the privilege and have to deal with the consequences of their actions regarding their anger. Remind them of the commitment to anger management they made originally when part of the group. This commitment should be upheld even though the group has ended.

In addition, if you face resistance from teachers regarding the contract, explain to them that it is meant as a technique/tool for anger management in an effort to be proactive instead of reactive. If a teacher feels a particular student will take advantage of the contract, agree to meet with the teacher and student together to go over the rules of the contract. Encourage teachers to give the contract a try—they may be pleasantly surprised! Tell the teachers that the contract may help them, as it allows a "time out" for a student who is very angry or "out of control" and this usually would take up much of their time. By using the contract, both the teacher and the student can effectively deal with the situation, with a minimal amount of time lost.

Coping Mechanisms (30 Minutes)

Tell the group that you are going to continue talking about coping mechanisms, and ask them to recall what the definition of *coping mechanisms* is.

"*Coping mechanisms*: Skills and ways of handling anger in a positive an effective manner."

Tell the group that the "Anger Management Contract" is a healthy way of handling one's anger. So it is a coping mechanism.

Ask the group, "What are some healthy ways of handling anger? In other words, how do you want to change your behaviors when you handle your anger?"

Make a list on the board titled "Healthy Ways to Handle Anger."

Tell the group that when they are experiencing an anger outburst, they should ask themselves the following three questions:

1. What am I feeling now?
2. Why am I feeling this way?
3. Where are these feelings coming from?

Ask the group to reflect on these questions and then add them to the chart as a coping mechanism.

Introduce some new coping mechanisms:

1. Choose constructive (not destructive) methods/solutions/ideas when dealing with anger.
   - Try physical outlets, such as working out, doing aerobics, playing sports, doing arts and crafts, painting or drawing a picture, dancing, or going for a run.
   - Problem solve and come up with action plans, such as forming a neighborhood watch for vandalism or crime.
2. Involve an objective third party. Ask someone you trust to intervene and help with the situation.
   - Explain to the group that this third party may be one of their "Safe People."
   - Explain to the group that involving an outsider for mediation or helping solve a problem is a good idea because sometimes you are too angry to see alternative perspectives. The third party should be someone who is *not* biased or involved in the conflict in any way. For example, if a student is angry because of a conflict with a teacher, a third party would be someone who was not present when the conflict occurred and can listen to both sides of the story—the teacher's and the student's. This would be an objective third party. Another student who is best friends with the student who is involved in the conflict with the teacher would *not* be an objective third party.
3. Write a letter to the person you are angry with. (The group may laugh at you when you suggest this, but I still urge you to suggest it.) Tell the group that this is just an exercise to release their angry feelings. The letter does not have to be sent. In fact, it can be ripped up and thrown out after it is written. The

option of sending it to the person they are angry with does exist though, and that can prove to be an effective form of conflict resolution, depending on how the letter is written and how the other person receives the letter.

4. Use relaxation techniques. Examples: guided imagery, deep breathing (as in the group wrap-ups), reading a self-help book, listening to a nature CD or other calming music, or taking a walk.

Wrap-up (Eight Minutes)

Tell the group that for this week's wrap-up you are going to use an anger management technique known as "guided imagery" (see also pp. 23, 25).

Guided Imagery

Tell the group that you will need complete attention and silence for the guided imagery to work.

Turn off all lights and ask the students to close their eyes and put their heads down on their table or desk. Tell the students to get into a completely relaxed position. They should uncross their legs and get comfortable in their chairs. Students can take off their glasses and should move any books or papers away so they can rest their heads comfortably in front of them. Tell the students that you will be talking to them and asking them questions, but they are not to answer back. In fact, they should be silent throughout the entire exercise so that they do not disturb other group members.

Begin the guided imagery. Tell the students to think of a safe place. This can be a place they have been to or one they have never visited before. Ask the students to think about the sights and smells of their safe place. Ask them who is at the safe place? Are they alone? Tell them to feel the warm sun on their backs or the water on their skin if they are outside. Maybe they smell the flowers or feel the fresh air on their faces. Maybe they are walking on the beach and can feel the sand in their toes. Maybe they are inside on a bed with 50 pillows and all they feel is complete softness.

Tell them to visualize their safe place and soak up all its sights, sounds, smells, and feels. Tell them to relax completely while they continue thinking about their safe place. Tell the group to move through their body, one muscle group at a time, tensing and releasing them. Start with the toes. Tell the group to curl their toes and release them, releasing all tension from their toes. Proceed to their legs and tell them to release all the tension from their legs by tightening and releasing the calf and thigh muscles. Move to their arms, their shoulders, and finally their faces, telling them to tighten and release each muscle group.

Bring them back to their safe place. Remind them that they are completely relaxed now and that all the tension from their body has been released. They should still be thinking of their safe place and its smells, sights, sounds, and feels.

Let the group sit in silence for 30 seconds, just thinking about their safe place. Then call them back and tell them to slowly come back to reality. Tell them to slowly open their eyes when they are ready.

TIP: The group should open their eyes before you turn the lights back on.

Turn the lights on and ask the group how they are feeling. Explain to the group that they can go to their imaginary safe place any time they choose. No one can ever take that away from them. When they are feeling very angry, going to their imaginary safe place can help them calm down. Explain that this is an example of a healthy coping mechanism.

Dismiss the group.

Before the next group, you should type up the giant list of coping mechanisms from the board and save it. You will add to it the following week.

After the group is finished, you should get all required signatures on the "Anger Management Contract" and sign them as well (if you haven't already). Make at least five copies of the signed contract. One goes in the student's binder/folder, one goes to the student to keep on them at all times, one goes to the principal or vice principal, one goes to you, and the last one(s) go(es) to the teacher(s) who will be involved in implementing the contract.

Don't forget to prepare for next week's session, which requires materials for a collage. Gather magazines, scissors, glue, and poster board.

Week 6

Note: For this session, you will need at least one big poster board, markers, glue, scissors, and magazines.

Check-in (Five Minutes)

Before getting into this week's content, you should check in with the students to see how they are doing. You do not have to ask each student individually; it should just be a general check in. "How's everyone doing? How has this week been so far? How was your weekend? Did anyone have any questions or reactions to last week's group?"

ANGER MANAGEMENT CONTRACT

This is a plan to help you when you start to feel angry or out of control. This is a plan to help you effectively manage your anger while in school. This is a privilege and is NOT to be taken advantage of.

SAFE PEOPLE I CAN TALK TO:

1. _____

2. _____

3. _____

SAFE PLACES I CAN GO:

1. _____

2. _____

3. _____

Student Signature _____

Social Worker/Counselor Signature _____

Principal/Administrator Signature _____

Teacher(s) Signature(s) _____

_____

This part should run smoothly and quickly. It's just a quick introduction, yet it makes the group come together and feel comfortable with each other.

Hand out binders/folders to each group member.

Contracts (Two Minutes)

Hand out signed contracts to each member and explain again that this is a privilege and *not* to be taken advantage of. The "Anger Management Contract" is a plan being put into place to help them handle their anger. If they abuse it, then they will not be using their newly learned effective coping mechanisms in handling their anger.

Introduce the Last Anger Management Coping Mechanisms (10 Minutes)

5. Work toward anger resolution through acceptance—learning to live with the fact that some people will *never* change.
6. Have realistic life expectations. Some people do *not* change, and there is nothing anyone can do about it.
7. Focus on the present as well as the future. Ask yourself what consequences your actions will bring.
8. Realize that some things are just *not* worth getting so angry or worked up about. Learn to let the small things go.
9. Learn to forgive people and yourself! Everyone, including you, makes mistakes. Forgive them! Forgive yourself and move on!

Collage (25 Minutes)

Tell the group that today they are going to use their creative sides and make a giant list of ways to deal with anger effectively. They can include what they have learned as well as other coping mechanisms that they think of on their own. The list can only include coping mechanisms that are *healthy* and 100 percent effective! Tell the group to be creative and cut out words and pictures from magazines and draw pictures on the poster board. It should be a collage when finished. (Ask the group if they want it to be hung up in the school halls for people to see.)

Wrap-up (Five Minutes)

Tell the group that you are going to do a relaxation exercise. Turn off the lights and ask for complete silence. Tell the group members to close their eyes and take a slow deep breath in through their nose and hold it in their mouth. Tell the group to release tension each time they exhale. Repeat this three times. Turn on the lights and ask the group how they are feeling. Dismiss the group and tell them you will see them next week at the same time. Tell the group that next week will be their last session.

Before the next group, you will add new coping mechanisms to the giant list of (created last session) and add them to the group member's binders/folders.

Note: Make sure *all* coping mechanisms are on the list, including the ones the group came up with last session, the ones you introduced last session and this session, and any new ones the group came up with and put in their collage.

Optional: Make certificates of achievement for each student for completing or graduating Anger Management. I use Publisher to make quick and easy certificates. They look nice, and the kids love them! It gives them a sense of accomplishment and achievement (see the sample certificate on p. 60; use color and be creative!).

Week 7

This is the last group. The pizza party and certificates for completing the group are optional but make for a nice celebration and termination.

Check-in (Five Minutes)

Before getting into this week's content, you should check in with the students to see how they are doing. You do not have to ask each student individually; it should just be a general check in. "How's everyone doing? How has this week been so far? How was your weekend? Did anyone have any questions or reactions to last week's group?"

This part should run smoothly and quickly. It's just a quick introduction, yet it makes the group come together and feel comfortable with each other.

Hand out binders/folders to each group member. Tell the group that this is the last time the Anger Management Group will meet. Tell them that they will find a list of "Healthy Ways to Manage Anger" in their binders/folders. Explain to them that today they can take their binders/folders home with them, and they should refer back to them constantly to continue their anger management on their own.

Tell group to take out the "Healthy Ways to Manage Anger" list and follow along with you (five minutes). Recap all anger management techniques and coping mechanisms. (The list should provide you with a description of each; otherwise, you can see previous sessions for explanations of each technique/coping mechanism.)

ANGER MANAGEMENT CERTIFICATE

CERTIFICATE OF ACHIEVEMENT

This certificate is awarded to

Name of Recipient

FOR THE COMPLETION OF A SEVEN WEEK COURSE IN ANGER MANAGEMENT

Signature

Date

Signature

Date

Tell the group that you, as the leader, have provided them with the necessary tools to handle their anger in a healthy and effective manner, but now it is up to them to take what they have learned and use it in their lives.

Talk about the group's feelings about the group ending (10 minutes).

Acknowledge the members for their commitment to the group, from start to finish, and congratulate them on their accomplishment of finishing the entire seven weeks.

Optional: Hand out certificates, eat pizza, and have fun!

STRENGTH EXERCISE (GRADES 3 THROUGH 12)

Materials: Index cards, markers/pens

Time: 20 minutes

Hand out index cards with one blank side. Instruct the students to write "Strength" on the blank side. On the other side, tell the students to write about a time they used a strength to overcome an obstacle.

Note: Make sure you explain what a "strength" is before the exercise. Say to the students, "A *strength* is a characteristic of your personality or something you are good at, not always a physical strength." Some examples are being a good listener, being good at sports, making good grades, being able to make friends easily, and so on.

Have students share with the group/class what they wrote and why. (Some may not want to share, and this is okay, but encourage most to share. Sharing with the group is powerful, and it is important to creating group cohesiveness.)

LETTER-WRITING EXERCISE (GRADES 5 THROUGH 12)

Materials: Paper, pens/pencils

Time: 45 minutes

Hand out loose-leaf paper and pens/pencils.

Tell the group that they will be doing a letter-writing exercise today and it may bring up some strong emotions, but they should try their best and not be ashamed or embarrassed if emotions come out.

Instruct them to write a letter to someone or something that has influenced their life. It can be a positive or a negative influence. Give examples such as a real person (like their mother, a friend, or their grandfather) or something nonhuman (like poverty, racism, or their learning disability).

During the letter writing, ask the group to remain silent and not talk to one another. This will help them concentrate and really work hard on their letters. Tell the group that they can spread out, sit on the floor, and so on while they write.

After the letter writing is complete, ask group members to share. (Be aware that their letters may address sensitive topics and that some members will not be willing to share. This is okay; however, try and encourage most participants to share as sharing can be quite powerful and therapeutic.)

Ask the group to reflect on the exercise and share their feelings. Dismiss the group.

Note: If a disclosure of abuse or another serious matter comes to your attention through this exercise, make sure you handle it effectively as a mandated reporter. Confidentiality and mandated reporting are discussed in chapter 7 ("Crisis Intervention—Protocol and Assessments").

SOCIAL SKILLS EXERCISE (GRADES 3 THROUGH 8)

Materials: Paper, pens/pencils

Time: 10 to 15 minutes (This exercise can be done as a class or in a small-group setting. It is great for the first day of class or as a team-building exercise.)

Tell the students to get into groups of three to five people (depending on if this is done in a large or small group).

Tell the participants to write down as many things as possible that they *all* have in common. Examples: favorite food, favorite TV show, all live in the same state, all have pets, and so on. Ask the students to write down things that are difficult, not just easy things. Make each student speak to every other student in the group.

Allow the student three to five minutes to complete the list.

Go around to each group and have them share what they came up with. The group that has the most and best answers wins a prize.

PREJUDICE EXERCISE FOR ADOLESCENTS (GRADES 6 THROUGH 12)

Materials: Chalk/dry erase board (optional—if you want to put the Prejudice Game on the board)

Time: 30 to 45 minutes

Tell the group they are going to do an activity about prejudice.

PREJUDICE GAME

Making fun of someone's weight

Not including someone because of their weight

Making fun of someone when they are reading

Joking with a friend

Believing that it is okay to hit guys but not to hit girls

Making fun of someone because they have an accent or don't speak English

Not being friends with someone because of their skin color

Thinking someone is stupid because they got a bad grade

Thinking someone is dumb because of their skin or hair color

Not letting a girl play with GI Joe dolls

Not letting a boy take dance lessons because he is a boy

Laughing at a little girl who is playing with trucks because she is a girl

Making fun of a girl who dresses in baggy clothes and has a short haircut

Calling a boy "gay" because he wears tight jeans or acts feminine

Ignoring someone because they are disabled or in a wheel chair

Ignoring someone because they are blind

Assuming that someone with a learning disability is stupid

Ignoring the new kid at school because they look different

Making fun of the kid who doesn't have new clothes and calling them poor

Not inviting a girl to your party because she wears different clothes than the other girls at school

Define *prejudice*: "*Prejudice*: Perceived opinion not based on reason or experience. To be biased."

Tell the students that you are going to discuss prejudice today and play the Prejudice Game. You are going to list several examples that may show prejudice or not. The students are to call out whether they think the example shows prejudice or doesn't. They do not need to raise their hands.

After the game, discuss what prejudice is and how it is not being fair to people: "Prejudice is thoughts *too*, not just actions." Discuss with the group their own prejudices and if they have ever experienced prejudice themselves. How did it make them feel? What would they do to change prejudicial thinking if they could?

DIFFERENCE EXERCISE (ELEMENTARY GRADES)

Materials: Index cards, markers/pens

Time: 30 minutes

Hand out index cards with two blank sides.

Have the students write the word "DIFFERENT" on one side.

Have the students write a few sentences about a time when they felt different on the other side. (You can use the words "prejudiced against" with older groups and "left out" with younger groups.)

Examples:

"I felt different when I came to this country because I spoke Spanish and everyone else in my class spoke English better than me."

"I felt different when all of my friends wanted to play sports and I wanted to play a musical instrument. I was told that boys only play sports."

"I felt left out when everyone with lighter skin color got picked for the volleyball team and I was left for last."

"I felt left out when all my friends were invited to Susie's party and I wasn't."

Have everyone share, and begin a discussion with the class about how being left out and different can be hurtful and is also known as "prejudice," "racism," and so on.

Ask the group members how it felt to feel left out or different. Discuss ways they can make sure that they don't intentionally leave someone out: "Invite a student who is sitting alone to sit with you at lunch. Don't spread rumors. Play with everyone at recess, not just your group of friends. Introduce yourself to a new girl or boy at school. Don't bully or make fun of someone who is 'different.' Accept difference as a good thing, *not* a bad thing."

DIVERSITY EXERCISE (GRADES 6 THROUGH 12)

Materials: Paper, markers/pens, chalk/dry erase board

Time: 30 minutes

Ask everyone to take out a sheet of loose-leaf paper and to *not* write their names on it.

Tell the students that you are going to talk about stereotyping and prejudice.

Define *prejudice* and *stereotyping*, or ask a student to define the terms:

"*Prejudice:* Perceived opinion not based on reason or experience. To be biased."

"*Stereotyping:* To negatively categorize a 'type' of person."

Give an example: "A negative stereotype is assuming that all blondes are dumb."

Then tell the students that you are going to mention a group of people, and they are to write down all the stereotypes associated with that group (use the "Groups" list on the next page).

Assure the students that these are not necessarily their thoughts or feelings—it is just what they have heard or been told. Tell the group that you want to get all the stereotypes and prejudicial comments and biases out in the open.

After the students have written down the stereotypes, ask for volunteers to read what they have written. Make a large list on the board.

Ask students to raise their hands if they have ever felt stereotyped against. Have they ever believed or used stereotypes against another person?

Lead a discussion about how believing in and following stereotypes and prejudices can be hurtful and harmful. Ask the students to reflect on the exercise and share their feelings. Ask them how they felt doing the exercise. Was it difficult? Uncomfortable?

Go around to each group member and ask what they can do to reduce stereotyping and prejudice. This may be difficult for the group members, especially if it is a younger group. Lead with an example: "I will reduce my own stereotyping by not participating in jokes that are prejudicial to others. For example, I will no longer tell 'blonde' or 'gay' jokes."

Tell the group they all did a good job participating in this difficult activity. Dismiss the group.

GROUPS

Asian people

Black people

Hispanic people

Jewish people

White people

People who are gay

People who are lesbian

People in wheelchairs

People with developmental or intellectual disabilities

Single fathers

Single mothers

Boys

Girls

GIRLS' LOVE AND HEALTHY RELATIONSHIP ACTIVITY (GRADES 9 THROUGH 12)

Materials: Poster board, markers, scissors, glue, magazines

Time: 45 minutes

Note: This activity is meant for an all-girls group.

Tell the girls they are going to do an activity about relationships, both healthy and unhealthy.

Ask the girls to make a collage using magazine pictures, words, and drawings to create what love and a healthy relationship looks like. Give examples: marriage, individuality, intimacy, commitment, loyalty, trust, affection, holding hands, and so on.

When the first collage is finished, ask the girls to make another collage. This time they will make a collage of what love and a healthy relationship is *not*. Examples could include violence, control, possession, jealousy, abuse, lack of independence, fear, and so on.

When both collages are done, ask the group members to reflect on each by sharing what the differences between the two are. Ask the group if they learned anything. Ask them to reflect on their feelings.

Dismiss the group. The posters can be hung in the social worker's office or be displayed in the hall at school. Ask the girls which they prefer.

GIRL BULLYING (GRADES 6 THROUGH 12)

Materials: Paper, pens/pencils (optional: *Mean Girls* movie, *Odd Girl Speaks Out* [Simmons, 2004] and *Queen Bees and Wannabees* [Wiseman, 2009] books)

Time: 30 to 45 minutes

This group should be small, with no more than eight to 10 girls. This exercise is meant for a group that has already been up and running for a few weeks. The group should be in the stage where it has formed some group cohesiveness and the comfort level and group rules have been established.

Tell the group that today you are going to talk about bullying between girls.

Guiding questions to help facilitate the discussion:

"How are girls different than boys in the ways that they are mean?"

"What do girls do to each other to be mean?"

"Is this bullying?"

"Why do people bully?"

"What's with the mean looks? What's with the rumors and exclusions from the group?"

"Why do girls hold grudges?"

"Why do girls just all of a sudden drop their friends?"

Talk about the movie *Mean Girls*. Read excerpts from *Odd Girl Speaks Out* and *Queen Bees and Wannabees* and get the group members' reactions and feedback.

TIP: Keep this part of the group about girls who bully in general. In my experience, girls have a lot to say about this topic if they feel removed from the situation and are not asked to speak about their personal experiences with bullying.

(The following exercise is optional. If you feel the group needs to take ownership of their actions as bullies, both past and present, this exercise can be very powerful. You have to gauge the group's feelings though, because if it isn't the right time to introduce this activity, you may be faced with resistance.)

Group exercise: Hand out paper and pens or pencils. Say to the group, "I want you all to write a letter to a person of your choosing. The person you choose can either be someone who has bullied you, someone you bullied, or a friend who you are no longer friends with. Maybe you miss this friend. Maybe you are glad you are no longer friends. Either way, I want you to write them a letter stating your feelings, whatever they may be: angry, hurt, missing them, and so on. Don't worry, you will *not* be sending this letter to anyone. This is just an exercise for this group. You don't even have to use the real name of the person you are writing to."

Ask for volunteers to read their letter. Reflect on the letters as a group. Ask group members for feedback and their thoughts about the letters.

Lead a discussion about what the group members can individually do to combat bullying between girls and what the school can do as a whole.

Examples:

Individually: Stop the spreading of rumors. Don't leave someone out. Make friends with many different "groups" or "cliques." Don't participate in gossip or mean teasing of others.

Schoolwide: Create a peer mediation program. Go to counseling. Report bullying and so on. (Effective interventions to combat bullying are covered in chapter 4 ["Workshops and School Programs"].)

In conclusion, tell the group, "This is your school. Make it yours. You want to be *part* of *one* group rather than several different groups. Why break up the school into many different groups? You are all students in *one* school—come together and make the school yours!"

Ask the students to reflect on the group and share their feelings. Dismiss the group.

BODY IMAGE EXERCISE FOR ADOLESCENT GIRLS (GRADES 6 THROUGH 12)

Materials: Poster board, markers, glue, scissors, magazines

Time: 45 to 60 minutes (can be varied to fit other time frames or done over two group sessions)

Note: This exercise is meant for an all-girls group.

Tell the group they will be doing an activity on body image today.

Ask the girls group the following question: "What does a health body look like?" Examples: Skinny? Overweight? Curvy? Skeletal?

Ask the girls to make their own individual collage or drawing of what they think a healthy body looks like.

After the collages/drawings are done, ask the girls, "What does a healthy body represent?" They can add these words to their collages/drawings if they want to.

Words should include things like the following: "healthy," "confident," "beautiful," "fit," "not skeletal," and so on. Redirect the girls if they use words like "fat," "gross," or "out of control."

Chapter 4

WORKSHOPS AND
SCHOOL PROGRAMS

This chapter includes sample workshops and programs that can be offered at your school. Each workshop is thoroughly explained, with a "how-to" section for implementing it in the school. The peer mediation program includes a week-by-week training guide to help train peer mediators. How to implement, run, and oversee the workshops and programs is explained in full detail. Workshops and programs in this section include antibullying and acceptance, conflict resolution, kindness, test anxiety, dropout prevention, and substance abuse and suicide prevention workshops as well as the peer mediation program.

ANTIBULLYING AND ACCEPTANCE WORKSHOP
(GRADES 3 THROUGH 8)

Materials: Pens, pencils, chalk board/dry erase board

Time: 45 minutes

Introduce yourself and tell students that you are going to do an activity about bullying.

Ask the students, "What is bullying?"

"*Bullying:* When one or a group of students make fun of another student for being different."

Hand out the "Bullying Survey" (see p. 75) All kids should take the survey individually, but they should *not* put their names on it. Make sure to tell the students this.

Collect the surveys from all students, shuffle and hand the papers out again randomly, and ask the students to raise their hands when the answer is "yes" on the sheet in front of them, *not* when that is what they wrote.

Make a chart on blackboard with students' answers. (Record the number of hands raised for each question on the board.)

Based on their answers, tell the students, "It seems like a lot of you have been bullied at some time."

Read the "Antibullying Quiz" aloud (see p. 76).

Ask the students to say "true" or "false" to each question. They don't need to raise their hands, they can just call out the answers.

Read the answers to quiz and ask the students, "Are you surprised? Did you know these answers?"

Move into a discussion about bullying interventions: "What can we do when we see people being bullied or are being bullied ourselves?"

Make a list on the board of all student answers. You should add appropriate interventions to the list, such as these:

- Tell a teacher.
- Tell a parent.
- Tell a counselor.
- Tell the principal.
- Stop the bully from being mean to other students.
- Don't participate when someone is being bullied (take the power away from the bully).
- Walk away.
- Don't participate in the spreading of rumors.
- Go to peer mediation or peer counseling.
- Repetition: Say "Leave me alone" repeatedly.

Tell the students what they should *not* do in regard to bullying:

- *Do not* fight back or get your friends to gang up on the bully.
- *Do not* bully other kids yourself.
- *Do not* keep it to yourself.
- *Do not* pretend it isn't happening or ignore it.

Conclude the intervention discussion by saying the following: "Remember, we need to be nice to each other.

"We need to respect each other. What is respect? What does it look like?"

Ask the students to give a clear definition of what respect is and looks like. (The definition of *respect* can change within different cultures and age groups.)

"Remember the Golden Rule: Treat people how you want to be treated! Don't ever forget that! I doubt any of you would want to feel put down or made fun of by another person. So be nice to others! Don't hurt others intentionally!"

Begin another discussion with the students regarding reasons why some students bully others.

Discussion Questions:

"Why do people pick on people who are different?"

"Why do you think some people bully others?"

"Why do you think people who witness others being bullied don't do anything about it? Do you think they are scared?"

"What does it mean to be popular? Is it okay to hurt others in order to be popular?"

"Do you think it is okay for a student to be scared to come to school because they are afraid of being bullied? Doesn't everyone have a right to an education?"

"We need to talk about difference and bullying and continue to talk about this."

"This is your school, let's make it safe and fun for everyone!! It's up to you guys!! We have to work together to stop bullies from bullying! Teachers, counselors, and principals can do their part, but you, as students, have to do yours too!"

Tell the students you are going to do an exercise before the workshop ends. This exercise is called the "Red Zone Exercise."

Red Zone Exercise

Ask the students to come up with a list of places in the school where bullying is more likely to occur. Write the list on the board. Examples are listed here:

- Gym locker room
- Hallways
- Buses

Tell the students that these areas are now going to be called the "red zone" areas. Notify teachers, administrators, and other students about these areas so that more staff can be placed at them. Also, encourage the students to say the words "red zone area" when they witness a student being bullied in one of them.

Closing Exercise What Do We Have in Common?

Have the students break off into groups of five.

Have all student in each group go around and tell something about themselves.

Next, have each group (by themselves) make a list of five to 10 things that everyone in the group has in common.

Share with the entire group.

Recap and remind the students what to do when they see someone being bullied or they themselves are being bullied.

Note: Make yourself available to students after the workshop for questions and private talks.

CONFLICT RESOLUTION WORKSHOP (GRADES 6 THROUGH 12)

Materials: Dry erase/chalk board

Time: 30 minutes

Introduce yourself and reveal the topic of the workshop: conflict resolution.

Explain to your audience that there are three common ways of dealing with conflict, but only one is truly effective.

"*Fight* (ineffective):

"This is when one person yells at another and the other person yells back. The argument escalates and turns into a full-blown fight. Each person feels defensive and attacks the other. Neither person can hear what the other is saying. No resolution is reached."

"*Flight* (ineffective):

"One or all of the people involved in the conflict leaves the situation and avoids discussion of the conflict. Continued avoidance of the situation is common. The people involved in the conflict may never even talk about it. They may even 'make up' without acknowledging that they had an argument previously. No resolution is reached.

"Note that removing yourself from a conflict when you are too angry and cannot communicate effectively because of the escalation of your anger is a healthy anger management technique. Later on, you will come back to discuss the conflict and reach a resolution. Do *not* confuse walking away when too angry to speak for the ineffective *flight* resolution."

"*Unite* (effective):

"This is when two or more people come together after they have cooled off and are ready to discuss the conflict. This is the most positive kind of conflict resolution. Both parties are calm and can let each other speak as well as actively listen to each other."

BULLYING SURVEY

DO NOT PUT YOUR NAME ON THIS PAPER! Please be as honest as possible.

Please answer yes or no to each question:

Has anyone ever called you a name? ❏ Yes ❏ No

Has anyone ever hit, kicked, or pushed you? ❏ Yes ❏ No

Has anyone ever told you that you can't be friends? ❏ Yes ❏ No

Has anyone ever threatened you? ❏ Yes ❏ No

Has anyone ever spread a rumor about you? ❏ Yes ❏ No

Has anyone ever made you feel bad about yourself on purpose? ❏ Yes ❏ No

Has anyone ever laughed at you in a mean way? ❏ Yes ❏ No

Has anyone ever made you sit alone at lunch time? ❏ Yes ❏ No

Has someone ever been mean to you because of how you look? ❏ Yes ❏ No

Has anyone ever made fun of you in a way that made you feel bad? ❏ Yes ❏ No

Did you tell anyone about any of these incidents? ❏ Yes ❏ No

Have you ever seen anyone else being bullied? ❏ Yes ❏ No

Have you ever stood up for someone that was being bullied? ❏ Yes ❏ No

Have you ever called anyone else a name, hit, kicked, pushed,
threatened, or been mean to someone? ❏ Yes ❏ No

Have you ever done or said something cruel because you were
afraid that if you didn't, you would be bullied or picked on? ❏ Yes ❏ No

Have you ever spread a rumor about someone or gossiped
behind their back? ❏ Yes ❏ No

(*Source:* http://www.tolerance.org/sites/default/files/documents/bully_early_handout1.pdf)

ANTIBULLYING QUIZ

Answer true or false to each question.

1.	Nearly 1/3 of American teens are involved in bullying.	True	False
2.	Fewer than 10 percent of American teens admit to bullying others.	True	False
3.	Students who are bullied are usually considered "nerds," "emos," or "weird."	True	False
4.	Most students who bully have low self-esteem and are insecure with themselves.	True	False
5.	Most bullies are bigger than the people they bully.	True	False
6.	Students who witness bullying usually try to make it stop.	True	False
7.	Most students who are bullied tell someone.	True	False
8.	A student who is being bullied should just ignore the bully and the bullying will stop.	True	False
9.	Bullies have trouble making friends.	True	False
10.	Most bullies grow out of bullying when they become adults.	True	False

---

1. True
2. False—most teens do admit to bullying others.
3. False—anyone can be bullied.
4. True
5. True
6. False—fewer than 10 percent of students who witness bullying do anything about it. Most ignore it or walk away.
7. False—most students who are the victims of bullying keep it to themselves.
8. False—ignoring bullying never works. It usually gets worse!
9. False—bullies make friends easily.
10. False—many bullies actually get arrested and end up in jail because of violent or aggressive behavior!!

(*Source*: http://www.tolerance.org/sites/default/files/documents/bully_upper_handout1.pdf)

"*Four things to remember after reaching the unite stage:*

"1. Give and take time to cool off: Each party needs their own amount of time to 'cool off' and revamp after the argument or conflict. Even if one party feels they are ready to discuss the conflict, the other party may not be ready yet. Do *not* rush the resolution. Be patient and wait for each party to become ready to communicate.

"2. Use 'I' sentences: Do not point your finger and blame others, as in 'You did this and that is why I am mad!' Instead, use 'I' sentences. For example, say 'I feel upset when I am not invited to your parties' rather than 'You never invite me to your parties.' That is an attacking statement and will provoke an attacking or defensive response. 'I' statements are not attacking and are your own feelings. No one can dispute your feelings. They are your own!

"3. Don't interrupt: When each party is ready to discuss the conflict, each person takes a turn to share their feelings and perspectives. One person talks without interruption, and then the next person talks. If one person has a question or reaction about what the other person has said, they *must* wait until it is their turn to speak. If this is not possible because of continued arguing or escalation of anger, perhaps more 'cool off' time is needed.

"4. Use feelings: No one can dispute your feelings. If you say 'My feelings were hurt when you . . .,' no one can say that your feelings weren't hurt. Your feelings are your own! Use them! Sharing your feelings is not attacking the other person, and it also provides perspective to the other person, who may not have been aware of your feelings to begin with."

Ask the students for reactions and feedback: "What do you think about the three ways of handling conflict? Can you identify which way you handle conflict? How can you change the way you handle conflict in order to get to the *unite* stage?"

Facilitate a group discussion.

DROPOUT PREVENTION WORKSHOP (GRADES 9 THROUGH 12)

Materials: Index cards, markers/pens, scissors and a chalk or dry erase board

Time: 45 to 60 minutes

Introduce yourself and the topic of the workshop: students dropping out of school.

Hand out index cards to the students and ask them to write their names on them to use as name tags. (If you know the students, you can skip this step.)

Ask the students to write on back of an index card why it is important to come to school. Ask for volunteers to share answers.

Tell the students you are going to ask them 10 questions (use the "List of 10 Questions" on the next page). Instruct them that they should raise their hand if they themselves or someone they know has ever felt any of these things.

After the students have raised their hands, acknowledge their answers. Most likely all of the students will have raised their hand at least once. Say, "Wow, so all of you raised your hand at least once! That means that each of you has one or more characteristics of a student at risk of dropping out of school! Does this surprise you?" Facilitate a short discussion, but be mindful of time as the workshop is meant to last less than or up to one hour.

Begin a discussion about dropping out of school. Ask the students, "What happens to students who drop out of school?" Facilitate a short discussion and then move on to the statistics portion of the workshop.

Ask the students, "Why do students drop out of school?"

Read the "Statistics of What Happens When Students Drop Out of School" sheet aloud (see p. 80).

After reading the statistics, move on to the scenarios section of the workshop. Ask the students to pair off into partners or groups of three. (They should just pair up with the person or people next to them so they are not running all over the room.)

Hand out scenarios (see p. 81). These should be precut into slips of paper, making them easy to hand out.

Instruct the students that they will read the scenarios silently in their group. Then one partner will read a scenario out loud, and the other partner(s) will say the reason the student is at risk for dropping out.

You should write all the reasons on the board. Ask the students, "Are there any other reasons that students drop out that you can think of?" Add these reasons to the list on the board.

Facilitate a discussion based on the list of reasons that students drop out of school. Ask for volunteers to share what advice they would give the students in the scenarios if they were their friends.

Hand out the "Resources for Students at Risk of Dropping Out of School Rank Sheet" (see p. 82).

LIST OF 10 QUESTIONS

1. Have you or someone you know ever felt like staying in bed rather than getting up to go to school?

2. Have you or someone you know ever received a bad grade?

3. Have you or someone you know ever repeated a grade or been left back in school?

4. Have you or someone you know ever felt that a teacher didn't understand you?

5. Have you or someone you know ever skipped a class or school altogether?

6. Have you or someone you know ever felt that you weren't as smart as the other kids in your class?

7. Do you consider yourself to be of African American or Hispanic origin?

8. Have you or someone you know ever disliked a teacher?

9. Have you or someone you know ever felt that you'd rather be working and making money than being in school?

10. Have you or someone you know ever felt that there was not enough time in the day to handle school and your other responsibilities?

STATISTICS OF WHAT HAPPENS WHEN STUDENTS DROP OUT OF SCHOOL

Students who drop out of school are more likely to receive public assistance and welfare in their adult life.

Students who drop out of school are more likely to end up in prison. In fact, 82 percent of U.S. prisoners have dropped out of school.

Students who drop out of school are more likely to end up as single parents.

People without a high school diploma earn an average of $12,000 per year, whereas a person with a high school diploma can earn an average of $25,000 to 50,000!

(*Source:* Statistic Brain, n.d.)

SCENARIOS

- Derek is a 16-year-old African American boy who lives in the housing projects in the inner city. He is very poor. He was recently given the opportunity to make a lot of money selling drugs. However, he has to sell the drugs during school hours and therefore misses school so he can make money.

- Kristen is a 15-year-old girl who recently became pregnant by her boyfriend. Kristen is constantly sick due to her pregnancy and has been missing a lot of school lately.

- Carl is a 14-year-old boy who has four younger brothers and two younger sisters. Carl lives in the housing projects with his single mother, who has severe arthritis and can't take care of the children. Carl's mother needs help taking care of his siblings. Carl makes it to school only one or two times a week as he has to stay home and care for his brothers and sisters on the days his mother is feeling ill.

- Jorge is a 17-year-old Hispanic boy who has not been to school in several weeks. The attendance counselor calls home and finds out that Jorge has been attending parties instead of going to school.

- Joe is a 15-year-old boy who is in special education. He recently repeated the ninth grade and is feeling like he is the dumbest in his class. Recently, Joe has stopped attending school.

- Alana is a 14-year-old girl who just broke up with her boyfriend at her school. Alana and her boyfriend are in several of the same classes. Alana is feeling very sad and doesn't want to get up in the morning to go to school because she is afraid she will have to face her boyfriend.

- Kara is a 16-year-old girl who is constantly getting into fights with her teachers. She feels she is not getting the right grades and that her teachers are too tough on her. She has missed three days of school this week.

- Tanya is a 13-year-old girl who has been being bullied by another group of girls. She is afraid to come to school and doesn't want to be made fun of. She has been pretending to be sick so that she gets to stay home.

- Luis is a 14-year-old boy. Luis's father recently got laid off from his job and asked Luis to stay home from school and work so that he can support the family until his father gets a new job. Luis has missed three weeks of school so far.

- Rose recently became an outcast with her friends. She is no longer allowed to sit with them at lunch and is not invited to any of their parties or gatherings. Rose is feeling very alone and like she wants to just drop out of school. She has been cutting school every day for the past week.

RESOURCES FOR STUDENTS AT RISK OF DROPPING OUT OF SCHOOL RANK SHEET

Please rank each from very helpful (1) to sometimes helpful (2) to not helpful (3).

TALKING TO A SCHOOL COUNSELOR/SOCIAL WORKER	1	2	3
TALKING TO A TRUSTED TEACHER	1	2	3
GOING TO PEER COUNSELING/PEER MEDIATION	1	2	3
TALKING TO A PARENT/RELATIVE	1	2	3

Instruct the students, "I am handing out a list of resources that could be helpful for students at risk of dropping out of school. You will see a scale of 1, 2, 3 next to each item. I want you to circle 1 for 'very helpful,' 2 for 'sometimes helpful,' and 3 for 'not helpful.'"

Ask the students to fill out the rank sheet by themselves. Give them a few minutes to do this. Then ask for their answers and why they chose those answers. For example, if a student tells you that they chose "3—not helpful" for talking to a parent or relative, ask what their reason was for their choice.

Make a list on the board titled "Resources for Students at Risk of Dropping Out of School." The list will include the choices the student felt were very or sometimes helpful.

Conclusion: Recap the reasons students drop out and the resources available to them. This will differ in each school. Maybe your school has a peer mentoring or peer mediation program. Perhaps your school has a dropout prevention or truancy counselor. Add these to the list of resources.

KINDNESS WORKSHOP (GRADES K THROUGH 2)

Materials: Paper, markers, crayons, bully book/story

Time: 45 minutes

Introduce yourself and reveal the name of the workshop: "Kindness Workshop."

Explain what *bullying* is: "Name calling, hitting, pushing, kicking, leaving someone out."

Read a story or tell a story about bullying. The story should be simple, such as one of a bigger boy stealing lunch money from a smaller boy, calling him names, or tripping him. This exercise is meant for very young kids.

Explain what performing a "kind act" is. More and more schools today are having "Kindness Days," and this exercise goes perfectly with that type of day.

"*Kind act:* doing something nice for someone else—for example, helping someone up when they have fallen, or carrying an old woman's groceries for her, and so on."

Ask the kids to come up with some more examples of kind acts.

Hand out blank pieces of paper, and have each student draw a picture of a kind act (doing something nice) or themselves doing a kind act.

Have every student share what they drew with the class.

Explain to the students that being kind is the opposite of being a bully. Bullies are usually mean to other people and rarely do kind things to others.

Tell the students, "Remember kids, we have to be nice to each other. We have to play with each other and not leave others out. If someone calls you a name or hits you or won't play with you, you *must* tell your teacher. Let's all try and do one kind act today!"

SUBSTANCE ABUSE WORKSHOP (GRADES 9 THROUGH 12)

Materials: Paper, pens/pencils, dry erase/chalk board

Time: 45 minutes

Introduce yourself and the topic of the workshop: substance use and abuse.

Read the "Statistics" sheet (see p. 85).

Begin a discussion with the students: "What do you think of those statistics? Do they scare you? Have you ever known anyone who has used or abused drugs or alcohol?"

Tell the students you are going to hand out an *anonymous* survey (see "Substance Abuse Survey," p. 86). They are *not* to put their names on it, and they are to do it by themselves.

After the students have completed the survey, collect the surveys, mix them up, and hand them back out randomly. Ask the students to raise their hands when there is a "Yes" marked on the paper in front of them. They are *not* to raise their hands for what they put on their paper. This keeps the exercise anonymous.

Acknowledge their answers and say, "Wow, it looks like many of you have or know someone who has used alcohol or drugs."

Read the "Effects of Alcohol and Substance Abuse" sheet to the group (see p. 87). Tell the students that these are just a few of the effects they may experience and suffer from by using drugs or alcohol. Facilitate a discussion about the dangers of these effects. Example: "Imagine you felt like you could fly because you were high on meth and you jumped off a building. You could get seriously injured or even die! What about the effect of becoming violent or aggressive? Can you imagine if you were hanging out with your boyfriend or girlfriend and all of a sudden they became aggressive or violent toward you because they were using alcohol or drugs? What would you do? How would you feel? Would you be safe?

"This is scary stuff, guys. You have to take care of yourselves and each other! If your judgment is impaired and you have difficulty making decisions, how can you take care of yourself or your friends?"

STATISTICS

25% of youths agree that a lot of drug selling occurs in their neighborhoods. One in six has been approached by someone offering them drugs.

One in five people ages 12 to 20 admits to being a binge drinker. Binge drinking is defined as having five or more drinks on one occasion.

Underage people who reported binge drinking are seven times more likely to use drugs than those who do not binge drink.

In 2010, one in seven teens reported using a drug that is considered an over-the-counter or prescription drug. The street name for these drugs is "pharmies," and they include drugs like Xanax, Klonapin, hydrocodone, and so on.

In 2000, one in 10 Americans reported driving while under the influence of either alcohol or drugs at least once in their lifetime.

55% of reported rapes occurred when the attacker was under the influence of drugs and/or alcohol.

(Source: Substance Abuse and Mental Health Services Administration, 2009)

SUBSTANCE ABUSE SURVEY

DO NOT PUT YOUR NAMES ON THIS PAPER! PLEASE BE AS HONEST AS POSSIBLE. THIS IS ANONYMOUS.

PLEASE ANSWER YES OR NO TO EACH QUESTION.

Have you ever been offered a cigarette?	❑ Yes	❑ No
Have you ever smoked a cigarette?	❑ Yes	❑ No
Have you ever drunk alcohol?	❑ Yes	❑ No
Have you ever been drunk?	❑ Yes	❑ No
Have you ever had five or more drinks at one time?	❑ Yes	❑ No
Have you ever passed out or blacked out from drinking too much?	❑ Yes	❑ No
Have you ever been offered to smoke marijuana?	❑ Yes	❑ No
Have you ever been offered other illegal drugs like cocaine, heroin, acid, or meth?	❑ Yes	❑ No
Have you ever tried other illegal drugs like cocaine, heroin, acid, or meth?	❑ Yes	❑ No
Have you ever been offered or tried over the counter or prescription drugs like Xanax, hydrocodone, or Vicodin?	❑ Yes	❑ No
Have you ever attended a party where there was alcohol and drugs available?	❑ Yes	❑ No
Have you ever felt pressured to drink alcohol or take drugs because if you didn't, you felt you might not be accepted or fit in?	❑ Yes	❑ No
Do you or have you ever had a friend who made you worried because of his or her alcohol or drug use?	❑ Yes	❑ No
Do you ever feel worried about your own drug or alcohol use?	❑ Yes	❑ No

EFFECTS OF ALCOHOL AND SUBSTANCE ABUSE

- Problems with memory and learning

- Loss of coordination

- Visual problems that make it difficult to drive or walk

- Difficulty thinking or solving problems

- Difficulty making good decisions

- Increased heart rate

- Depression

- Increased or decreased appetite

- Hallucinations—hearing or seeing things that aren't really there

- Becoming angry or irritable

- Becoming violent or aggressive

- Nausea

- Sweating a lot

- Feeling like you are invincible—like you can do anything (for example, that you can fly)

Recap about the survey: "So you guys said that you either use or know someone who has used alcohol and/or drugs. Now that we know the dangers that abusing alcohol and drugs can cause, what do we do to prevent it?"

Ask the students what they think they can do to help a friend who has a drug or alcohol problem. Ask them what they would do if they felt that they themselves had a drug or alcohol problem.

Make a list of interventions on the board:

- Talk to a school counselor/social worker.
- Talk to the principal.
- Talk to a parent, older sibling, or adult relative.
- Talk to a trusted teacher.
- Tell a parent/teacher or counselor about a friend who is using drugs or alcohol
- Tell your friend to get help.
- Call 911 if you are somewhere and your friend passes out or is acting strange due to the effects of drugs or alcohol.
- Say *no*—if your friend is offering you a drug and you don't want it, say no. If they are your true friend, they will accept you whether you take the drug or not.

"*Important—tell someone!* If you are worried about yourself or your friend and think you or they might have a problem with alcohol or drugs, tell someone!! Help is available! Do *not* keep it to yourself!"

Note: Make yourself available to students after the workshop for questions and private talks.

SUICIDE PREVENTION WORKSHOP (GRADES 6 THROUGH 12)

Materials: Paper; scissors; markers; dry erase/chalk board; two signs: one that reads "MYTH" and another that reads "FACT" (the signs need to be big enough for the students to read them from far away)

Time: 45 to 60 minutes

Introduce yourself and reveal the topic of the workshop: suicide prevention.

Myths and facts: Say to the group, "I want to go over some myths and facts about suicide.

"Everyone please stand up. I am going to read several statements about suicide, and you are going to decide whether you think the statement is a myth (false) or a fact (true). You will go to the MYTH sign and stand in front of it if you think the statement is a myth. You will go to the FACT sign if you think the statement is a fact."

Put up the signs that say "MYTH" and "FACT."

Have each student go to the MYTH sign or the FACT sign when you read a statement.

Statements (read the answer after each statement and send students back to their seats or the middle of the classroom before proceeding to next statement):

1. Suicidal people have full intention of dying. Nothing anyone says or does can stop them. (MYTH)
   Most people who have suicidal thoughts or feelings desperately want help but don't know how to ask.
2. Suicide happens without warning. (MYTH)
   There are almost always warning signs before a person takes their own life.
3. Improvement in a suicidal person means the danger is over. (MYTH)
   Many suicides occur months after the beginning of improvement. When a person is normally withdrawn or sad all the time and then all of a sudden happy, it is a danger sign.
4. People who talk about suicide do not commit suicide. (MYTH)
   Most people who take their lives talk about it first to at least one person.
5. Suicide occurs in all races, ethnicities, and social classes. (FACT)
6. Only "emos" or crazy people commit suicide. (MYTH)
   All types of people commit suicide—all ages, races, sizes, ethnicities, and so on.
7. Asking a person if they are thinking about killing themselves will trigger them to actually taking their own life. (MYTH)
   Most people who are contemplating suicide are desperately seeking support and understanding. Asking could actually save a life!

Read the "Statistics" sheet to the group and ask for their reactions (see p. 90): "Did you know that suicide is this common? What do you think or feel when you hear the word 'suicide'?"

Read the "Warning Signs" for suicide to the students (see p. 91). Ask the students to share their reactions to the warning signs. Did they know them before you read them? Did they learn anything new?

Move on to what they should do:

"Tell someone!! If you have, or someone you know has, thoughts of hurting or killing themselves, you *must* talk to a trusted adult.

STATISTICS

Each day, more than 1,000 American teenagers attempt suicide. Of those, 18 will actually die.

95% of teen suicide is preventable! This means it can be stopped!

Suicide is the number 3 killer for people ages 10 to 24.

Teen suicide is more common than cancer, heart disease, influenza, stroke, pneumonia, and chronic lung disease *combined*!

Teen suicide is more common than homicide.

One in five teens has thought about suicide, and one in 10 has attempted it.

Teen boys are more likely to commit suicide, but teen girls attempt many more times.

(*Source:* National Institute of Mental Health, 2010)

WARNING SIGNS

Look for these warning signs among your friends and family members:

Suicide threats, direct and indirect:
   "I wanna kill myself." (direct)
   "They will be sorry when I'm gone. I won't be here anymore." (indirect)

Obsession with death: drawings, poems, journaling, MySpace or Facebook images and pictures, always talking about death

Dramatic changes in personality: used to be really happy, now withdrawn and sad

Loss of interest in activities: used to like soccer, now doesn't play anymore; doesn't seem to care about the things they used to love

Overwhelming sense of guilt or shame; blaming themselves; always thinking everything is their fault

Changes in eating or sleeping habits: If your friend tells you that they wish they could sleep all day or isn't eating lunch anymore, these could be warning signs of depression.

Drop in school performance: used to get good grades, now failing every class; doesn't seem to care about homework anymore

Giving away belongings: If your friend offers to give you something that means a lot to them, this is a big warning sign. They could be planning on killing themselves.

Previous suicide attempts: If you know someone who has tried it before, they could still be at risk.

Having a plan: If you or someone you know has thought about killing themselves and they have a plan, tell someone immediately—you could save their life!

"I know your friends mean the world to you, and they may tell you not to tell. But you'd rather have a friend who is mad at you and alive than a friend who is dead.

"Tell a school counselor, your parent, a teacher, the principal, a family friend, or a trusted friend who will tell an adult for you. *Do not keep it to yourself!!* Most people do not tell, and this is why every 18 minutes a teen kills themselves!!"

If you are a teacher or staff person and you think a student is at risk for suicide or exhibiting the warning signs, talk to the school counselor, social worker, or principal. Call the parent. Do *not* ignore the warning signs or depressed behaviors. If you speak up, you may *save* a child's life!

"If someone tells you they are thinking of killing themselves or are feeling depressed, do *not* judge them.

"Listen to them and offer help.

"Take them to the school counselor or a trusted teacher. Tell them you will go with them."

Hand out the "Resources" sheet (on the next page). You can add local resources to the list when you teach the workshop at your school.

Suicide is a sensitive topic. It may be wise to end the workshop with some deep breaths or a relaxation exercise as chances are emotions will be high (see the relaxation and deep breathing exercises in chapter 2).

Note: Make yourself available to students after the workshop for questions and private talks.

TEST ANXIETY WORKSHOP (GRADES 3 THROUGH 8)

Materials: Dry erase/chalk board

Time: 30 to 40 minutes

Introduce yourself and reveal the topic of the workshop: test anxiety or, for younger kids, worrying about taking a test.

Ask the group as a whole, "What do you feel when you know a big test is coming up?

"What happens to your body?

"You may begin sweating, get chills, or shivering. Maybe your heart races. You may get tense all over your body. Maybe you tense your shoulders, bite your nails, or even have racing thoughts.

RESOURCES

1-800-SUICIDE: 24-HOUR NATIONAL HOTLINE

[Give out resources pertinent to the location where workshop is presented.]

911 FOR AN EMERGENCY

"These things happening in your body are called *cues*. Cues can cause you to react and do things like worry, have trouble sleeping, get a stomach ache, not want to go to school, and tell yourself you are stupid or going to fail.

"It is important to notice your body cues, because then you can do something about how you react to them!

"So the next time you notice body cues like sweating, biting your nails, or feeling tense about an upcoming test, do the following:

"Do some deep breathing (in through your nose, hold for five seconds, and then slowly release through your mouth).

"Take a break from studying.

"Go to extra help or tutoring with a teacher.

"Do guided imagery [this is discussed in chapter 2].

"Think about something else when you are feeling really tense (for example, a happy memory, a joke, something funny you recently saw on television).

"Only look at the clock three times during the test.

"Turn the clock around, or place it out of your view if you are at home and having trouble sleeping the night before a test."

"Talk to or call a friend to distract yourself from feeling nervous or tense about your upcoming test.

"Tell yourself that you can do it! Believe in yourself!

"Tell yourself that you are prepared because you studied!

"Don't let yourself worry about the exam after a certain time at night. Actually say to yourself, 'I am not allowed to worry or think about the test after 8:00 P.M. tonight!' Do the best you can on the day of the test. That is all you can do!

"When getting the test back, tell yourself that you tried your best and whatever happens, you are still a smart and good person!"

PEER MEDIATION PROGRAM: TRAINING AND IMPLEMENTATION (MEANT FOR HIGH SCHOOL, BUT COULD BE USED IN MIDDLE SCHOOL)

Materials: Paper, pens, markers, folders/binders, chalk/dry erase board

Time: 30 to 45 minutes weekly for eight weeks

Peer mediation is an excellent tool for promoting conflict resolution in schools. In fact, statistics show that schools that have peer mediation programs have less violence in than do other schools (see http://www.nationalsave.org/). Other benefits of peer mediation include the following:

- creating a safe and open-minded culture,
- teaching students how to handle conflict in healthy ways,
- teaching students of different backgrounds to work together, and
- offering an alternative to traditional disciplinary interventions.

Implementing a peer mediation program in your school requires a lot of well-thought-out work. Whenever beginning a peer mediation program, the necessary groundwork—including pitching the program to your administrator, leading professional development training for teachers, completing the recruitment and selection process for mediators, and conducting the eight-week training for student mediators—must have been completed beforehand. A step-by-step process of how to create and implement a peer mediation program in your school is provided in this section.

Step 1: Program Startup

As mentioned in chapter 3 ("Group Implementation and Counseling Activities"), communication with your administrative staff is essential before starting any new program at your school. To review your understanding about program startup, I encourage you to go back and look at chapter 3, specifically the material on how to create and implement groups. Peer mediation—although a program, not a group—should be implemented in a manner similar to the formation of a group.

With the understanding that you have thoroughly reviewed the material on how to implement a group, only a shortened version of it is provided here.

To begin the process of implementing a peer mediation program in your school, you should first meet with your administrators to pitch the idea. Because peer mediation is meant to be a form of disciplinary intervention, I would advise you to go fully prepared to the meeting with your administrator. Be prepared when the principal asks you how peer mediation will help with conflict resolution and how it will fit into your school's code of conduct. Most administrators welcome new ideas for interventions regarding discipline, but some may be quite strict in their view of discipline and will not want to see peer mediation as the only disciplinary intervention option. My advice is to propose peer mediation as an intervention program, *not* a disciplinary program.

During this meeting, you will also want to establish a location where peer mediation will take place. It may be able to take place in your office, depending on the size, or it may need to take place in a conference room or unused classroom.

After meeting with your administrator(s) and getting their approval to begin the program, your next step is to get teachers and school staff on board. A full professional development session about peer mediation should be conducted for teachers. The presentation should include what the program is about, what it is meant to accomplish, how it will help your school, the selection of peer mediators, the training that mediators will receive, and the referral process when the program is actually implemented (you can find this presentation in chapter 5 ["Communicating with Teachers and Professional Development"]).

After getting the support and approval from your administrators and teachers, it is time to get the interest of students. This can be done by posting flyers about peer mediation around the school, asking homeroom teachers to make announcements and hand out flyers, or simply spreading the word to students you know and work with.

Before posting flyers or making announcements, you must define the criteria of what you envision your peer mediators to be like. In other words, if you are only looking for peer mediators who are in the 11th or 12th grade, that should be included in the flyer or in your announcement. The application process could be included in the flyer as well—things like the fact that each prospective mediator will need to fill out an application and have an interview with you to become a peer mediator. Or you can simply spread the word about recruitment for the program and make it a requirement that any student who is interested comes and speaks with you. I would caution you not to include *any* descriptors, however, because then your office may be flooded with students. You may just want to put one or two requirements on the flier, such as must be in 11th or 12th grade or available after school, and so on.

Step 2: Application Process

After you have created student interest, the application process should begin. You should visualize exactly how you would like students to apply to become mediators. Will you require an application only? Will reference letters from teachers be required? What about an interview with you? You may want all of these to ensure the best selection of peer mediators. Your peer mediators need to be responsible, compassionate, and good students. The training to becoming a peer mediator is extensive, and you don't want students who are not fully committed to the cause, including the time commitment. Create an application that clearly states the requirements for becoming a peer mediator and what the process will entail. Remember the requirements you put in the flyers are to attract student interest. The application is where you can get specific about those requirements (a sample application appears on the next page).

PEER MEDIATOR APPLICATION

REQUIREMENTS:

Must be in 11th or 12th grade

Must not have any recent disciplinary infractions

Must be in good academic standing (passing all classes)

Name _____ Grade _____

1. I want to be a peer mediator because:

2. List personal qualities that will help you be a good peer mediator:

3. Please obtain two signatures from teachers, administrators, or staff who recommend and support you becoming a peer mediator:

Staff Signature _____

Staff Signature _____

If selected, as a peer mediator I agree to the following terms:

I will complete all required training and follow-up sessions.
I will serve as a peer mediator as scheduled by the school social worker.
I will request peer mediation when I need to resolve my own conflicts.
I will make up any missed class assignments during peer mediation training or duty.

Signature _____ Date _____

PLEASE RETURN TO SCHOOL SOCIAL WORKER'S OFFICE NO LATER THAN: [DATE]

If you do want to make interviews a requirement, put that on the application as well. Then tell the students that after review of the applications, interviews will be conducted. Interviews can help you get to know those students who have applied who you may not know well. They will also provide an opportunity for you, as the school social worker, to explain what becoming a peer mediator entails and for the students to ask questions about the program.

Note: This is the time to think about how many peer mediators you will need and accept. My advice is to keep it limited to about 10 to 15 students, especially if this is your first time implementing a peer mediation program.

Step 3: Inform Teachers, Staff, and Students about the Training

After the application and selection process is complete, you need to inform students, teachers, and the administration of the who, where, and when of peer mediation. The *who* refers to the students who have been selected to begin training to become peer mediators. First, you need to inform the students whether they were chosen or not. For students who were not chosen, give an explanation of why. It could be as simple as they didn't meet the requirements or that you had too many applicants and the selection process was very difficult. Tell the students that there will be other opportunities for them to apply to be mediators in the future as the program will be ongoing.

The *where* refers to the location in which peer mediators will meet, both for training and to conduct mediations. (Remember, this has to be mutually agreed upon by you and your administrator).

The *when* refers to the time of day the training will take place. The training is eight weeks long and, therefore, needs to occur on a weekly basis. As mentioned in chapter 3, getting feedback from teachers about the time of day you will conduct the training is always a good idea. Remember that you will *not* be able to accommodate *all* needs. Try to schedule the trainings when the students have lunch or a free period to limit their missed class time. Another option is to speak with the physical education teacher or another elective teacher who may grant the students permission to miss class once a week. Either way, always clear it with your administrator first.

Step 4: Training (Eight Weeks)

Materials: Paper, pens, markers, folders, binders

To run an effective peer mediation program in your school, you must conduct extensive training of peer mediators. Meetings should occur weekly and run for about 30 to 40 minutes. A week-by-week training program is outlined here.

Week 1

Welcome the group and congratulate them on being selected as the first group of peer mediators for your school.

Introduce yourself to the group and tell them that you are going to meet for the next eight weeks to help them to become trained peer mediators. After the intensive eight-week training, the program will be implemented, and the times that you will meet as a group will vary, but you will most likely not meet on a weekly basis.

Have the group members introduce themselves, each stating their name and why they wanted to become a peer mediator.

Explain to the students that because the training is so time-consuming, it is important that they be committed to becoming mediators and all of the work it entails. To show their commitment to becoming a mediator, tell them that you have created a contract that you will request that they sign. Hand out the contract (see p. 101), explain the importance of commitment to becoming a mediator, and answer any questions regarding the contract. Collect contracts from every student and put them in the folders you will hand out to each of them.

Hand out folders. Let the students design the outsides of their folders with markers. Tell the students that they must write their name large and in the middle of the cover of the folder. Tell the group that the folders will be kept in your office for confidentiality reasons and that students will get their folders each week during training. After training is complete, these folders will serve as the mediators' personal files for the mediations they conduct. Each time they conduct a mediation, they will get their folder, which will contain all information needed for the mediation. This is confidential information, and that is why it will be kept in your office.

Begin training by explaining what peer mediation is and what it accomplishes.

What is peer mediation?

Peer mediation is the use of a peer mediator to help settle a dispute and reach an agreement between two or more opposing parties without the intervention of staff.

Some goals of peer mediation:

- To enable students to take responsibility for peacefully resolving disputes without the intervention of staff
- To increase the ability of students to deal effectively with issues of cultural and social diversity

- To prevent disputes from escalating into incidents that require disciplinary action
- To create a school climate that is characterized by cooperation, safety, and collaboration

When is it used?

Peer mediation is used when two or more parties cannot reach an agreement and are causing disruptions in class or in other people's lives.

Examples of when people may go to peer mediation:

- Two students have been fighting or are planning on fighting.
- One student is bullying another student (sometimes peer mediation isn't recommended for bullying—it depends on the situation).
- Students in class cannot or will not work together.
- Racial problems exist between two or more students.
- Friends are quarreling or fighting.
- Students are stealing from one another.
- Students cannot reach an agreement over an issue or problem.
- A student has received a referral from an administrator for disciplinary infractions.

Tell the students that peer mediation is a voluntary process and will not work if the disputing parties do not want to participate in it. Prior to conducting a mediation, peer mediators *must* make sure that disputing parties have agreed and want to participate in the mediation.

Roles of the mediator:

To uphold confidentiality: Tell the students that it is *very* important that, when they conduct a mediation, they keep what is said to themselves and only share it with you or other mediators during group mediation discussions. They are *not* to go and tell their friends or boyfriend or girlfriend what they heard or discussed during a mediation. Tell the students that if they break confidentiality, this will be grounds for dismissal from the program. The mediator should begin a mediation by explaining confidentiality to the students involved so that they feel comfortable participating in the mediation.

Discuss the times that confidentiality needs to be broken: suicidality, homicidality, child abuse disclosure, and whenever a mediator feels uncomfortable. Because

PEER MEDIATOR CONTRACT

As a peer mediator, I understand that my role is to help students resolve conflict peacefully. As a peer mediator, I agree to the following terms at [School Name]:

1. To complete all training sessions at the scheduled time.

2. To maintain privacy/confidentiality for all mediations.

3. To be a responsible peer mediator by conducting mediation sessions according to the process, completing all necessary forms, and promoting the program.

4. To come to peer mediation myself when I am unable to resolve a conflict on my own.

5. To make up any class work missed during training or mediations and to keep my grades up.

6. To serve as a peer mediator for the entire year.

Student Signature _____ Date _____

peer mediators are in a room alone with other students and usually not with staff, it is important that mediators knows when it is a time to stop a mediation and get the school social worker.

Note: Although you are not required to be present during a mediation, you should always be close by to answer questions or intervene when problems arise. Peer mediation is student driven but is *not* intended to occur without staff supervision.

Other roles of the mediator:

- To remain impartial
- To not be racially or prejudicially biased
- To facilitate communication between parties
- To help mediating parties reach an agreement that they both can live with (which may not be either party's ideal)

This last role embodies the main goal of peer mediation—to have opposing parties reach an agreement that they can live with. The entire reason students come to peer mediation is to resolve a conflict.

Collect folders and dismiss group until next week.

Week 2

Welcome the students back to week 2 of training.

Hand out folders to students, which should contain some loose-leaf paper on which they can take notes.

Tell the students that this training session will discuss sensitive material and may evoke some strong emotions. It is important to be open and honest about the emotions the students may feel and to discuss them. To be a nonbiased, impartial mediator, each student must be able to feel comfortable talking about issues that may make them feel uncomfortable, such as racism, prejudice, and so on. This way, if they are ever faced with these issues during mediation, they will know how to handle their own feelings.

Do the "Racism/Prejudice Activity" on the next page with the group (see chapter 3 for other stand-alone activities on this topic that can be done in groups).

After activity is complete, check in with the students about how they felt about doing the exercise and their concerns or anxieties about handling sensitive issues like racism and prejudice during mediations.

Collect folders and dismiss the group until next week.

RACISM/PREJUDICE ACTIVITY

Ask everyone to take out a sheet of loose-leaf paper and to *not* write their name on it.

Tell the students that you are going to talk about stereotyping and prejudice.

Define *stereotyping* and *prejudice,* or ask a student to define the terms.

"*Prejudice:* perceived opinion not based on reason or experience. To be biased."

"*Stereotyping:* to negatively categorize a 'type' of person."

Give an example: "A negative stereotype is assuming that all blondes are dumb."

Then tell the students that you are going to mention a group of people, and they are to write down all the stereotypes associated with that group (use the list of "Groups" from chapter 3 [see p. 66]).

Assure the students that these are not necessarily their thoughts or feelings, it is just what they have heard or been told. Tell the group that you want to get all the stereotypes and prejudicial beliefs and biases out in the open.

After the students have written down the stereotypes, ask for volunteers to read what they have. Make a large list on the board.

Ask students to raise their hands if they have ever felt stereotyped against. Have they ever believed in or used stereotypes against another person?

Lead a discussion about how believing in and following stereotypes and prejudices can be hurtful and harmful. Ask the students to reflect on the exercise and share their feelings. Ask them how they felt doing the exercise. Was it difficult? Uncomfortable?

Go around to each group member and ask how they would handle stereotypical and prejudicial remarks in a mediation situation. Acknowledge their anxieties regarding these issues. Remind them that, as mediators, they are to remain impartial and nonbiased, and if they are working with someone who they may feel uncomfortable with, they should seek out your assistance. In addition, if a comment that is racist or prejudiced is made during a mediation, they should redirect the comment by intervening and saying, "We are here to resolve a conflict and reach an agreement that is mutually agreeable to both of you. We are not here to call names or degrade each other." If they are unable to get the students back on track to reaching a resolution of their problem, it may be appropriate to end the mediation and reschedule it for another time when both students are willing to listen to the mediator rather than call each other names.

Week 3

Welcome the students back to week 3 of training and hand out the folders.

Tell the students that now that you have established the beginning level of comfort in being a mediator, you are going to get into the "bulk" of what mediators do and how to become an effective mediator.

Emphasize that to be an effective mediator, you must be an effective listener. It is okay to interrupt or redirect at times, especially if the opposing parties begin to argue or take over the mediation, but mediators are there to facilitate the process. At times they will need to intervene and run the process; however, mediators should not do most of the talking during a peer mediation session.

The mediator decides who speaks first—usually the person who suggested peer mediation. If the mediation was suggested by neither party, the mediator decides. One person speaks at a time. If the other person tries to speak, the mediator *must* intervene and tell that person that they need to wait their turn and that they will have an opportunity to speak soon.

"Always start mediations by introducing yourself and explaining the process as well as confidentiality."

Example: "Hi. My name is Alison. I am going to be your peer mediator for today. Peer mediation is when two or more students come together to get help from a student, like me, to resolve a conflict they are having and reach an agreement. Each of you will have a turn to speak, but I ask that only one person speak at a time and that when one person is speaking, the other remain silent and let that person finish. I know this may be difficult, but just remember that you want to be heard as much as the other person does, so allowing the other person to speak without you interrupting them will allow you to have your turn to speak without being interrupted. At times, I may stop you and ask questions, but I will try to keep my interruptions to a minimum. After you each speak, we will brainstorm ideas on how to resolve the issue you are struggling with. We will then reach an agreement and write it down on a contract that both of you will be asked to sign. I will ask that both of you keep what we talk about in here completely confidential and not tell anyone else, including your friends, about what is said here. I will also agree to that. However, there may be times when I have to get the school social worker and speak with them about what is talked about in here. Those times include when one of your reveals the desire to hurt yourself or one another or that someone is hurting you. You two may find that it is really difficult to reach an agreement, and then I will need to ask the school social worker to come in and help you reach an agreement. The whole point of peer mediation is for me to help you both reach an agreement that you can live with. Do you have any questions regarding what I just said? Can you both agree to the terms of mediation, such as confidentiality and not interrupting one another?"

Tell the students that this is just an example and that they don't have to say exactly what you just said to them. They just need to explain the process of peer mediation and make sure to include confidentiality. The more mediations they conduct, the better at giving an introduction they will become.

Teach Active Listening:

Active listening is when the students involved in a mediation really feel they are being listened too. That means that peer mediators are not daydreaming, texting on their cell phones, doodling, or so on. Tell the students that they signed up to be peer mediators because they wanted to help others, so they need to portray that to the students who come to mediation.

Give an example: "Imagine you went to get extra help from a teacher on your class work, and the entire time the teacher was talking on their cell phone and ignoring you. How would that make you feel? Students who come to mediation want to feel like they are being listened too.

"So, how do you become an active listener?

"By using these active listening tools:

"*Attending*: These are little encouragers, like 'I see,' nodding your head, 'go on,' 'uh huh,' 'okay.'

"*Summarizing*: This is repeating, rephrasing, and making clear what one person said. This makes it clear to the mediator and both disputing parties what the problem is. Make sure you are very clear! If you don't have a clear understanding of what the problem is, keep asking questions until you can clearly make a clarifying statement. For example: 'Correct me if I'm wrong, but you seem to feel that Jose doesn't listen to you when you are speaking? Is that true?

"'It seems to me that you feel ignored by Jose when you are trying to speak to him.

"'You just said that Jose never listens to you when you are trying to make a point, is that how you feel?'

"*Clarifying*: This is asking open-ended questions to get a full understanding of an issue.

"Here's an example: 'What did you want to do when Jose copied your homework? How does it make you feel when Jose copies your homework?

"'What does copying Maria's homework do for you, Jose?

"'What would happen if you both got caught cheating?'

"Try to avoid *why* questions. These can be perceived as attacking and can close down communication."

Role Play:

Ask for two volunteers to act as disputing students who have come to peer mediation. You, as the school social worker, will be the peer mediator and use all the active listening tools to portray how it should look during a mediation. Make sure you start off with an introduction and explain the peer mediation process, as mentioned.

Make up a conflict that might be encountered in peer mediation.

Use all active listening tools during the role play:

- Attending
- Summarizing
- Clarifying

Now, turn to the students and let them break into groups of three—two students being the opposing parties coming to mediation and one being the peer mediator. Remind the students to begin with an introduction and then practice using the active listening tools. You assign scenarios to the groups:

Scenario 1

Jose is constantly copying Maria's homework, and Maria is afraid of getting caught by the teacher but doesn't know how to tell Jose to stop copying.

Scenario 2

Matthew and Diego want to fight because Diego saw Matthew holding hands with Diego's girlfriend.

Scenario 3

Rene is always picking on Derek and making Derek give him his lunch money. Derek is very upset. He has gone to his teacher but feels that there hasn't been any change, so he wants to confront Rene in peer mediation.

Remind the students that they are only practicing the active listening tools and are not trying to reach an agreement yet. The role play should only last a few minutes, but real mediations will last longer. These tools allow the mediator to gather all of the information needed to later reach an agreement. If the mediator does not have a clear understanding of what the problem is, it will be very difficult to reach a resolution.

Teach DO NOT *in Peer Mediation:*

Tell the students that they should not do the following:

- Interrupt (unless redirection is needed, as explained earlier)
- Offer advice
- Share their own experiences, biases, or beliefs—the mediation is not about the mediator it is about the students involved in the mediation.
- Judge the students involved in the mediation regardless of their actions
- Criticize the students

Create a DO NOT and DO sheet for peer mediators to add to their folders (see next page).

Collect folders and dismiss the group until next week.

Week 4

Welcome the group back for week 4 of training and hand out folders.

Explain difference between single mediators and co-mediators:

"*Single mediator*: one peer mediator meeting with opposing parties alone to reach an agreement.

"*Co-mediator*: Two peer mediators meeting with opposing parties together. When conducting a co-mediation, peer mediators must define their roles by deciding which mediator will take an active role and which mediator will take a passive role. In other words, the active peer mediator will facilitate the discussion as if they were conducting a single-mediator mediation. The passive peer mediator is mainly there for support and to ask additional questions if the active peer mediator needs help."

Begin Teaching Peer Mediation Steps 1 through 6:[1]

Tell the students that there are six main steps to conducting a mediation and that you will cover three today and three next week:

---

[1] These steps are derived from Schrumpf, Crawford, and Bodine (1997a, 1997b).

DO NOT:

INTERRUPT (UNLESS REDIRECTION IS NEEDED)

OFFER ADVICE

JUDGE

CRITICIZE

SHARE YOUR OWN EXPERIENCES OR BELIEFS

DO:

MAINTAIN GOOD EYE CONTACT WITH EACH STUDENT INVOLVED IN THE MEDIATION

USE YOUR ACTIVE LISTENING TOOLS

REMAIN IMPARTIAL AND NONBIASED

ALLOW ONE PERSON TO SPEAK AT A TIME

FACILITATE POSITIVE COMMUNICATION

INTERVENE WHEN OPPOSING STUDENTS ARE BECOMING NASTY OR ARE CALLING EACH OTHER NAMES

GET THE SCHOOL SOCIAL WORKER WHEN YOU FEEL UNCOMFORTABLE OR HAVE QUESTIONS

BREAK CONFIDENTIALITY WHEN A THREAT OF VIOLENCE OR HARM IS PRESENT

1. *Agree to mediate:*

The choice has been made whether to do a single mediation or co-mediation, and a time and place where mediation can be done has been arranged (with your help). Tell the students that the referral process and setup of mediations will be explained after training is complete.

2. *Gather points of view:*

Use your active listening skills (review the active listening tools from week 3 if necessary).

Assign one person to speak at a time. The mediator may ask questions to clarify and summarize. Give an equal amount of time to each person.

This is where anger, hurt, and other feelings can comes out. Active listening is *very* important, but you also must be able to calm each party down if the discussion becomes too heated.

Make sure you do not allow the mediation to turn into a ranting session. Cut the parties off if need be. You *do not* want one party going on and on about how the other party is awful or not willing to make changes.

Keep the parties focused on the issue or problem that brought them to peer mediation: "For example, if two students come to mediation because Jose is copying Maria's homework, they should be focusing on that issue alone. If one or both students start bringing up other issues, bring them back to the issue at hand. Your job is to help the disputing parties reach an agreement about the conflict that brought them to peer mediation."

3. *Focus on interests:*

Ask questions such as these: "What is it that you want to get out of this? How would you like to see this resolved?

"What are you willing to compromise or sacrifice to reach an agreement?"

Point out where the two parties may agree: "Both of you said that you don't really want to get caught cheating for copying each other's homework. Let's talk more about that."

Role play steps 1 through 3. Assign scenarios to groups, some with single mediators and some with co-mediators. The students should use what they have learned up to this point, including the active listening tools. They should always start by introducing themselves and the process of peer mediation.

Scenario 1

Jose is constantly copying Maria's homework, and Maria is afraid of getting caught by the teacher but doesn't know how to tell Jose to stop copying.

Scenario 2

Matthew and Diego want to fight because Diego saw Matthew holding hands with Diego's girlfriend.

Scenario 3

Rene is always picking on Derek and making Derek give him his lunch money. Derek is very upset. He has gone to his teacher but feels that there hasn't been any change, so he wants to confront Rene in peer mediation.

Collect folders and dismiss group until next week.

Week 5

Welcome the group back for week 5 of training and hand out folders.

Review peer mediation steps 1 through 3 from week 4 and ask the students if they remember each step.

Teach Peer Mediation steps 3 through 6:

4. *Create win–win options:*

Brainstorm options for resolving the conflict. This is when peer mediators ask the disputing students to begin thinking about how they can resolve their problem. Example: "What can we do to fix this problem?"

The peer mediator writes down all ideas that the disputing students come up with on a sheet of loose-leaf paper from their folder.

Tell the students, "Do not comment on or judge ideas—just write them all down. If one party doesn't agree with some of the ideas, tell them that it is okay. You are just gathering ideas. Write down as many as possible."

5. *Evaluate options:*

The mediator asks each party to cross off and circle the ideas they like and are willing to try and the ideas they are not willing to try.

Cross off ideas that both are unwilling to try, and circle ideas that both are willing to try. Leave ideas that one party is willing to try but the other one isn't unmarked. You can discuss these options later and maybe reach an agreement.

When crossing off and circling, ask questions like this: "Is this option fair for both of you? Can you, and are you willing to, do it?"

Tell the mediators the following: "If you have trouble reaching an agreement, remind the disputing students that the agreement may not be ideal for both of them—it only needs to be tolerable and something they can agree to try."

6. *Create an agreement:*

When an option is chosen that both parties like or feel is fair, the mediator writes the agreement down and reads it aloud to both parties.

Example: "You both agreed that Jose copying Maria's homework is going to get you into trouble and may cause you to fail the class. You both agreed that you are willing to work together and help each other when doing assignments but not just copy. Is this correct? Do you still agree?"

The peer mediator then has each student sign a written agreement.

Hand out the "Peer Mediation Agreement" (see p. 112).

After the agreement is signed, the mediator should check in with each party and ask if the problem has been solved and if there are any unresolved issues regarding the current problem.

The mediator should then shake hands with each disputing party. If the mediator chooses, they can ask the disputing parties to shake hands with each other as well.

The mediator keeps the written agreement and puts it in their folder. A copy of the agreement can be given to the disputing students on their request.

Collect folders and dismiss the group until next week.

Type up a "Cheat Sheet" (see pp. 113–114) before the next group meeting and put it in all the students' folders so they will have it to review before conducting a mediation.

Week 6

Welcome the group back for week 6 of training. Tell them they are doing a good job and that, although it is a lot of information to take in, they *will* get it. Tell them you have created a "Cheat Sheet" for them that they will find in their folders. This can be used to review the active listening tools and steps of peer mediation before beginning a mediation. Tell the students that their first mediation will be difficult and they will probably be nervous, but the more mediations they do, the more comfortable they will feel and the easier the mediations will be to do.

Review steps 1 through 6 of peer mediation by asking the students what they remember. Don't allow them to look at the "Cheat Sheet" unless necessary.

PEER MEDIATION AGREEMENT

Date _____

We participated in a mediation. We have reached an agreement that we both believe is fair and solves the problem between us. In the future, if we have problems that we cannot resolve on our own, we agree to come back to mediation.

Name_____   Name_____

Agreement _____

_____

_____

_____

_____

_____

_____

_____

_____

Signature _____   Signature_____

Peer Mediator Signature _____

Co-Peer Mediator Signature_____

CHEAT SHEET

ACTIVE LISTENING TOOLS

ATTENDING: LITTLE ENCOURAGERS: "I SEE," NODDING YOUR HEAD, "GO ON," "UH HUH," "OKAY"

SUMMARIZING: REPEATING AND REPHRASING WHAT THE SPEAKER SAID: "IT SEEMS TO ME THAT YOU FEEL UPSET WHEN JOSE COPIES YOUR WORK, SINCE YOU JUST SAID THAT IT MAKES YOU MAD WHEN JOSE COPIES YOUR WORK."

CLARIFYING: ASKING OPEN-ENDED QUESTIONS: "HOW DO YOU FEEL ABOUT THAT?" "WHAT DOES COPYING MARIA'S HOMEWORK DO FOR YOU, JOSE?"

CHEAT SHEET (CONTINUED)

PEER MEDIATION STEPS

1. *AGREE TO MEDIATE:* SET DATE AND TIME FOR MEDIATION TO OCCUR

2. *GATHER POINTS OF VIEW:*
   - INTRODUCE YOURSELF AND EXPLAIN PROCESS OF PEER MEDIATION, INCLUDING CONFIDENTIALITY AND ITS LIMITS
   - ASSIGN FIRST PERSON TO SPEAK
   - USE YOUR ACTIVE LISTENING TOOLS
   - GIVE EQUAL AMOUNTS OF TIME TO EACH PERSON

3. *FOCUS ON INTERESTS:*
   - KEEP THE PARTIES FOCUSED ON THE ISSUE THAT BROUGHT THEM TO PEER MEDIATION. ASK QUESTIONS SUCH AS THESE: "WHAT DO YOU BOTH WANT TO GET OUT OF THIS?" "HOW DO YOU THINK YOU TWO CAN RESOLVE THIS ISSUE?"
   - POINT OUT WHERE THEY START TO AGREE: "YOU BOTH SAID YOU DON'T WANT TO GET CAUGHT CHEATING."

4. *CREATE WIN–WIN OPTIONS:* BRAINSTORM RESOLUTIONS TO THE CONFLICT. WRITE DOWN ALL IDEAS

5. *EVALUATE OPTIONS:*
   - MEDIATOR CROSSES OFF IDEAS BOTH PARTIES CANNOT AGREE TO AND CIRCLES IDEAS BOTH CAN AGREE TO. LEAVE OPTIONS ONE CAN AGREE TO AND THE OTHER CAN'T AS UNMARKED AND COME BACK TO THEM LATER
   - ASK PARTIES IF ONE OF THE CIRCLED OR UNMARKED OPTIONS IS FAIR FOR BOTH PARTIES

6. *CREATE AN AGREEMENT:*
   - WHEN AN OPTION IS CHOSEN THAT BOTH PARTIES AGREE IS FAIR, MEDIATOR WRITES THE AGREEMENT DOWN ON PEER MEDIATION AGREEMENT FORM AND READS IT ALOUD TO BOTH PARTIES
   - BOTH PARTIES AND MEDIATOR SIGN THE AGREEMENT
   - MEDIATOR SHAKES HANDS WITH BOTH PARTIES AND ASKS EACH PARTY TO SHAKE HANDS WITH THE OTHER

Role Play Full Mediations:

Assign scenarios to groups, both with single and co-mediators. Tell the students they are going to conduct a full mediation using all six steps, including coming to an agreement and filling out the "Peer Mediation Agreement."

Note: Make sure you have made enough copies of the "Peer Mediation Agreement" for the students to practice with.

Scenario 1

Jose is constantly copying Maria's homework, and Maria is afraid of getting caught by the teacher but doesn't know how to tell Jose to stop copying.

Scenario 2

Matthew and Diego want to fight because Diego saw Matthew holding hands with Diego's girlfriend.

Scenario 3

Rene is always picking on Derek and making Derek give him his lunch money. Derek is very upset. He has gone to his teacher but feels that there hasn't been any change, so he wants to confront Rene in peer mediation.

After each group role plays, they should share what they came up with as a resolution on the "Peer Mediation Agreement."

Discuss any issues or problems that may have occurred during the practice mediations.

Collect folders and dismiss the group until next week.

Week 7

Welcome students back to week 7 of training and hand out folders.

Review the six steps of peer mediation, allowing students to look at the "Cheat Sheet" in their folders. Answer any lingering questions and concerns the students may have about conducting a mediation.

Teach Caucusing and When to Get the School Social Worker:

"*Caucusing*: when the mediator meets with the disputing parties individually prior to the mediation. This is helpful when two parties are unable to reach an agreement or when the parties are too upset or angry to meet.

"By meeting individually with each party first, the mediator can get a full understanding of the problem. Caucusing also allows each person to feel heard and express their anger and hurt.

"Eventually, the caucusing will end, and the two parties will face each other in mediation. Remember that the goal is to reach a mutual agreement between parties."

Note: Tell the students that if they feel there is a need for caucusing before the mediation occurs, they should get you and discuss the situation. In addition, there may be times when you, as the school social worker, feel that caucusing would be beneficial prior to a mediation. In this case, the mediator would be notified of the reason for caucusing.

Tell the students that although they will be conducting the mediations alone or with a co-mediator, you will always be close by and available.

Review When to Get the School Social Worker During a Mediation:

- Confidentiality must be broken (suicidal ideation, homicidal ideation, disclosure of child abuse)
- You don't know what to do or you feel uncomfortable
- You feel unsafe
- There is yelling or fighting between the opposing parties
- The parties can't reach an agreement
- One party is not cooperating or is too angry to participate in the mediation process
- There are more than two students who want to mediate
- A student and teacher mediation is requested
- One or more of the students says they do not want to participate in the mediation (remember that peer mediation is voluntary, not mandatory)

Peer Mediator Availability:

Ask the students to write down their free times during the school day, including lunch, study hall, free periods, gym, and other electives that they may be allowed to be excused from to conduct a mediation. Because the need for a mediation is not predictable, there is no way of knowing exactly when a mediator will be needed. Tell the students that notice will be given about a mediation as far in advance as possible.

Explain the Referral Process for Mediations:

Show students the "Peer Mediation Request Form" (see p. 118). This form will be kept in your office as well as given to teachers, staff, and administrators. Teachers, administrators, and students can all make referrals for peer mediation. In fact, it is most effective when a student self-refers for help with resolving a conflict they have with another student.

"Peer Mediation Request Form"s will then be returned to you, and a peer mediator will be assigned on the basis of availability and fit for mediation.

Peer mediators will be assigned each week, unless a mediation is urgent and needs to take place immediately.

Peer mediators will be notified if they have been assigned a mediation by locating their name on the "Peer Mediation Schedule" (see p. 119), which will hang on your office door. Only the name of the assigned peer mediator(s), the time, and the date will be on the schedule so as to protect the confidentiality of the students involved in the mediation. Information regarding the mediation will be in the assigned mediator or mediators' folders, which will be kept in your office.

Tell the peer mediators that it is their responsibility to check your office door on a regular basis—at least once a week—to see if they have been assigned to conduct a mediation.

If they are assigned to conduct a mediation and it is during a class period (which you will make every effort not to do), the student must request permission to miss class. All work will be made up, and you will speak to the teacher if necessary.

Note: Most mediations will and should occur during a peer mediator's free periods, but this can't always happen, especially in the case of an immediate need for mediation.

Collect folders and dismiss the group. Tell the mediators next week is last group before the implementation of peer mediation!

Week 8

Welcome the peer mediators back to their final week of training.

Congratulate them for completing an intense and long eight-week training. Give out "Certified Peer Mediator" certificates (see p. 120).

Tell the students that although training is now officially over, you will continue to meet every other week to discuss mediations and problems and questions that arise as well as continue to hone their mediation skills.

Implementing the Program:

Tell the students that, as peer mediators they, need to promote peer mediation in order to let the school know about this new program.

Hand out pamphlets (see pp. 121–122 for sample) and ask the mediators to hand them out as well and post them around the school.

PEER MEDIATION REQUEST FORM

After filling out this form, please return to school social worker. Social worker will fill out the bottom portion and return it to the people involved in mediation.

Person requesting mediation _____

Date/Time _____

Students involved in mediation

Times available for mediation (Check and please write time)

❏ Morning Homeroom_____

❏ Lunch _____

❏ Afternoon Homeroom _____

❏ Elective _____

Reason for mediation: _____

_____

_____

_____

PLEASE DO NOT WRITE BELOW: SOCIAL WORKER MUST FILL OUT

Assigned Peer Mediator_____

Date/Time of Mediation_____

STUDENTS INVOLVED IN PEER MEDIATION SHOULD REPORT TO THE SCHOOL SOCIAL WORKER'S OFFICE AT _____ .

PEER MEDIATION SCHEDULE

Assigned Mediator	Date	Time/Period

PEER MEDIATORS, PLEASE REMEMBER TO CHECK YOUR FOLDERS FOR INFORMATION ABOUT THE MEDIATION.

PEER MEDIATION CERTIFICATE

NAME OF STUDENT

Has completed an 8 week intensive training course and is now a

CERTIFIED PEER MEDIATOR

FOR SCHOOL NAME

Signature

Date

Signature

Date

PEER MEDIATION PAMPHLET

PEER MEDIATION

STUDENTS HELPING STUDENTS

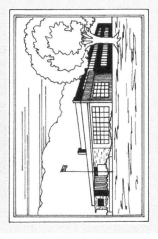

For more information or to request a mediation, please see

[School Social Worker's Name]

[School Social Worker's Contact Information]

Having a Conflict with Someone?

Has anyone made fun of you or teased you?

Did someone say, "Just wait until I get you after school"?

Is there a rumor about you going around school that you think someone started?

Are you in a fight with a friend?

Do you have a problem with someone that you can't seem to solve?

If you answered yes to any of these situations, you should

COME TO PEER MEDIATION!

PEER MEDIATION PAMPHLET (CONTINUED)

PEER MEDIATION

What Is Mediation?

Mediation is a chance for two disputing parties to sit face-to-face and talk, uninterrupted, so that both sides can be heard. After the problem is defined, solutions are created and then evaluated. When an agreement is reached, a contract is written and signed by all parties.

What Is a Student Mediator?

A student mediator is a peer who has been trained to conduct mediations. The student mediator facilitates fair and concise communication between disputing parties. Your fellow students were selected to help you resolve conflicts in a fair and helpful way.

What Are the Rules in Peer Mediation?

To make the process work, there are a few simple rules:

1. Mediation is a process that both parties agree to.
2. Everything said during the mediation remains confidential. What is said in the room, stays in the room.
3. In mediation, students take turns talking—no interrupting.
4. The student mediator never takes sides.

If I Have a Conflict, How Do I Go about Getting It Mediated?

It is very easy to request mediation. You can pick up a request form from the school social worker, [School Social Worker's Name]. Please fill it out and return to [School Social Worker's Name]. You will then be assigned a peer mediator and a time and place to meet.

Why Should I Try Mediation?

There are *many* reasons that you should try mediation, but here are just a few:

1. Conflicts that do not get resolved often end in fights, which could result in your being suspended.
2. Conflicts that do not get resolved often result in hurt feelings, which could cause you to lose friends.
3. You will learn to choose peaceful, responsible, and fair ways to solve your own problems without an adult doing it for you.
4. Mediation will help you and the other person develop mutual respect and clear communication.
5. Mediation will make [School Name] a more positive place to learn and grow.

Have the students make flyers and posters to promote the program and put these around the school as well.

Assign a few students to announce the implementation of peer mediation over the PA system (principal approval should be obtained prior to announcement).

Review the referral process and remind students that their folders will be kept in your office, the master schedule will hang on the door, and they should to check it weekly.

Collect folders and dismiss the students.

Step 5: Implementing/Running Peer Mediation

Now that you have completed the entire program startup process—which included pitching your program to administration, training teachers and staff, conducting the intensive eight-week training program for mediators, and promoting the program—it is time to implement and run the peer mediation program.

For the program to run smoothly, it is important to anticipate some problems that may arise and how to effectively handle them if they do.

Problem 1: Referral Management

Managing referrals appropriately is important. Handle the referral process for peer mediation in a manner similar to the way you handle referrals for social work services (review the referral process outlined in chapter 1). Not all referrals will be deemed appropriate for peer mediation. Use your clinical judgment when determining appropriate referrals for peer mediation. Inappropriate referrals may come from anyone—including teachers and administrators, not just students. For example, if a request for peer mediation comes in from a teacher regarding several girls picking on another female student, it's most likely that this is not a situation that is appropriate for peer mediation. The female student who is being picked on will most likely feel ganged up on. Usually, peer mediation involves two students or equal numbers of students on each side. In other words, four students is okay if there are two opposing parties on each side. Four against three is never appropriate for a mediation. Educating the teacher who sent you the referral is important, as is taking action to address the situation. Although the referral may not be appropriate for peer mediation, as the school social worker, you have just been notified of a potential bullying situation and the need to address it.

In managing referrals, it is also important not to feel too overwhelmed. When a new program is implemented, many times it takes off right away, and you may find yourself with too many referrals—many that are not appropriate for peer mediation. If this happens, first take a deep breath and relax, and then set up a meeting with staff to reeducate them about what an appropriate referral for peer mediation is. It may have been awhile since you led the professional development training for teachers, and they may need a refresher course.

So, we have talked about what to do when you receive inappropriate referrals; now we need to address what to do when you receive appropriate referrals. The peer mediation referral process was thoroughly explained in step 4, but I want to touch on the handling of these referrals. I would set aside a certain time or day of the week to go through referrals and assign mediators. Of course, there may be times when an immediate mediation is needed, so a quick glance when you first receive a referral won't hurt.

However, most referrals are going to be about ongoing problems and will be able to be scheduled in the future, such as in a few days or the following week.

Remember the schedule that we discussed in chapter 1? Add the peer mediation time to your schedule. Allow yourself time to go through referrals and time to be available when mediations occur.

Note: You can add peer mediation time to your schedule in the spots you left available for crises or paperwork. You don't have to be sitting around doing nothing while students are conducting a mediation, but it is best practice not to be conducting a counseling session during this time, just in case a mediator needs your assistance.

Problem 2: Confidentiality Breaches of Peer Mediators

No matter how many promises they make or contracts they sign, teenagers have difficulty keeping things confidential. Even though you stressed the importance of confidentiality of mediations to the peer mediators during the eight-week training, there still may be times when a mediator goes and tells a friend about a mediation they conducted. Accidents and slip ups occur. Even in our own practice, we reveal personal information about our clients to our loved ones. However, in a small school setting, it is really, really important to try to maintain the confidentiality of the students involved in a mediation. Students come to mediation to be listened to, and they trust the mediators to help them with their conflicts. If they feel they can't trust the mediators, they won't come, and the program will fall apart. Discussion of the paramount importance of maintaining confidentiality can be accomplished through ongoing training meetings with the peer mediators. However, if you hear that a peer mediator is not keeping their part of the bargain about the confidentiality of mediations, it is important to speak with them privately and immediately. Be supportive, and give the student a chance to come clean about breaking confidentiality. It may have just been a mistake, or it may be something entirely different, such as gossip or revenge. If the latter is the case, the situation must be dealt with between you, as the social worker, and the peer mediator. If you feel that the mediator will not be able to uphold the confidentiality of future mediations, unfortunately, it is probably best to dismiss them from their duties.

Problem 3: Mediations Resulting in Not Reaching an Agreement

Many times, especially in the beginning, peer mediators will request the assistance of the school social worker because they are unable to get the opposing parties reach an agreement. Assistance from you at this time is appropriate. It will serve two purposes: (1) Hopefully, it will help the two opposing parties reach an agreement, and (2) it will allow the peer mediator to learn how to effectively resolve a conflict in a difficult situation. Usually, as peer mediators become more comfortable with themselves *as* mediators, they will be able to resolve more conflicts and reach more agreements, and they will require less assistance from you.

Ongoing training of peer mediators should occur to help hone their mediation skills. These meetings will also allow for further role plays to review the steps of mediation. Mediators will have the opportunity to ask questions and discuss difficult mediations as well as to request feedback from each other and from you. It is important for you, as the school social worker, to encourage the peer mediators to support one another by offering feedback regarding their experiences of mediation. If, in the beginning, the peer mediators are having trouble conducting mediations, reaching agreements, and so on, it may be beneficial for you to sit in during the mediations. However, because peer mediation is meant to be student driven, those involved in the mediation must first agree to allow you to be present. As discussed in training, all students involved in mediation know that there may be a time that you will have to intervene; but having you present from the start is different and needs to be discussed in advance with all parties involved in the mediation.

As with any new program, problems and conflicts will arise. Take them in stride and deal with them effectively. Make mistakes, embrace them, learn from them, and move on to make the program better. You will see, as the program continues to run and you continue to make improvements, that it will turn out great! Peer mediation is one of the most effective conflict resolution programs out there, so give it a try!

Chapter 5

COMMUNICATING WITH TEACHERS AND PROFESSIONAL DEVELOPMENT

This chapter is about communicating with teachers. It covers effective communication techniques, including what to do and what not to do. Professional development presentations on bullying, behavior management, and peer mediation as well as tips for teachers working with certain types of students are included.

COMMUNICATING WITH TEACHERS

When speaking with teachers about students or your role as a social worker, or when providing professional development, abide by one rule: *Join* the teacher. Do not go against them. I am not saying that you shouldn't make suggestions or offer a different opinion to teachers in certain cases. I am simply saying that you should join them in their effort to help the student. Too often, I have seen a rift created in schools between the teachers and the school social workers. It saddens me, because essentially both are there for the same reason: to ensure student success. However, the rift exists in many schools. My advice in working with teachers is to listen to them, support them, and offer necessary suggestions. Many social workers see their role as a helper to the teacher but forget that the role is reciprocal. Teachers are with the students all day long, every day, whereas the social worker may work with a student or group of students only on a weekly basis. One of our many jobs as school social workers is to communicate with teachers. To be the most effective in your communication, I advise you to be supportive and to actively listen to teachers. More often than not, the social worker approaches the teacher with many different ways the teacher can help the student. But often the social worker neglects to listen to the teacher first. The social worker needs to remember that the teacher has 20 other students in the class and is not just one-on-one with the student, as the social worker usually is. The teacher often fails to hear what the social worker suggests simply because they are fed up with the student and don't know what to do. So, many intervention talks occur between the social worker and teacher when one or both professionals are at a heightened state of emotion. Either a teacher seeks out the social worker because "Johnny won't listen in class and I've had it with him!" or the social worker seeks out the teacher because the teacher is failing to implement Johnny's behavior intervention plan. In my experience, when emotions are high, nothing gets resolved. The best way to deal with this type of situation is for the social worker and teacher to meet at a convenient time for both, when they are feeling calm and prepared to talk.

When I worked in a school where a rift existed between the teachers and administrators, I was often asked by other social workers how I got along so well with the teachers. My answer was and still is this: It's all about the approach. If you approach a teacher and offer your help and expertise while listening to their concerns, the conversation will go well. If you approach the teacher in an attacking manner, the teacher will become defensive, and nothing will get accomplished. Remember why you and the teacher got into your professions: to ensure the success of students! Following are two examples of approaches to communication with teachers:

Effective approach to communication with teachers:

Social Worker: Hi Ms. Smith. I have some concerns about a student named Johnny in your second period math class. Would you be willing to meet with me to discuss my concerns?

Teacher: Sure. I'm free now.

Social Worker: It has come to my attention that Johnny has been having behavior problems in your class.

Teacher: Oh my gosh, Johnny is the worst! He is always late, so unorganized, and always disrupting my class.

Social Worker: It sounds like Johnny is causing you some difficulties in your class.

Teacher: You got that right! I've tried everything with him! He is such a pain!

Social Worker: Would you care to elaborate on what you've tried?

Teacher: I called home and gave him detention three times. Nothing works, though! I don't know what else to do!

Social Worker: Sounds like you have been trying very hard with Johnny and he just isn't responding how you would like him to. Maybe I can offer a few suggestions of ways to help you deal with Johnny's behavior.

Teacher: Please! I don't know what else to do, and I'm so fed up with him. I *do* want to help him—he is a sweet boy. Maybe I've been too hard on him. Anything you can offer would be greatly appreciated.

Ineffective approach to communication with a teacher:

Social Worker: Hi Ms. Smith. I have some concerns about Johnny, in your second period math class. You know who I'm talking about.

Teacher: Oh my gosh, Johnny is the worst! He is always late, so unorganized, and always disrupting my class."

Social Worker: I know Johnny very well, and he never gives me any problems. Maybe it's your teaching that he doesn't like.

Teacher: What? I'm a great teacher. You don't know what it's like to teach. You just take the kids and chat with them for 30 minutes.

Social Worker: I know how to help you with Johnny. Why don't you try this: _____.

At this point, the teacher and the social worker have become defensive, and neither is willing to listen to each other. The conversation stops, and Johnny is the one who suffers.

Notice that in the first approach, the social worker expressed the need to speak with the teacher but also asked if it was an appropriate time. In the second approach, the social worker just began the conversation with the teacher. In the first approach, the social worker listened to the teacher first and asked what she had tried before beginning with the interventions. Often social workers are so eager to offer the interventions, they forget to listen to what the teacher has tried already. The first approach showed the social worker joining the teacher in her difficulties with Johnny. Many times, teachers feel defensive when the social worker approaches them. They may feel that the social worker is there to criticize their teaching or classroom management. Social workers often feel looked down on by teachers or as though they have to continually justify their job to teachers. Through use of an effective approach, as shown in the first example, both the teacher and social worker can feel at ease when communicating and get back to the task at hand: ensuring the success of the students.

PREVENTION AND INTERVENTION STRATEGIES TO COMBAT BULLYING PROFESSIONAL DEVELOPMENT

Materials: Antibullying Quiz, PowerPoint, dry erase/chalk board, pens/pencils, paper, scissors, cut-out scenarios

Time: One to two hours

Introduce the topic of the professional development training: prevention and intervention strategies to combat bullying. This professional development workshop is mainly lecture based, but it includes activities and group discussion.

TIP: You may want to create a PowerPoint presentation with the information included as a visual aid for your audience.

Start by passing out paper and pens or pencils to all teachers. Tell the teachers you are going to read questions from an antibullying quiz (see p. 76), and they are to write down whether they think each answer is "true" or "false." Instruct the teachers to do this by themselves; it is not a test, just a measure of their knowledge about bullying.

After the quiz, reread each question with the answer attached. When an answer is false, a reason should be given. Ask the teachers if they were surprised by some of their answers. Did they get most of them right? Wrong?

Give a definition of *bullying:*

"*Bullying:* to use superior strength or influence to intimidate (someone), typically to force someone to do what one wants."

What Does Bullying Look Like?

- Teasing, calling names, public embarrassment, intimidation, spreading or creating rumors, forcing someone to sit alone at lunch or recess, laughing/whispering in an obvious manner, pointing and laughing when someone walks by, a group making fun of an individual
- Shoving, hitting, kicking, fighting, pinching, physically hurting someone (for example, "wedgies")

What Bullying Is Not

- Joshing or teasing between friends, when you can see friends smiling or having fun
- When the teasing appears harmless and the student does not seem distressed, it is most likely not bullying.

- Usually between one or two boys or girls, *not* a large group teasing an individual (that is bullying)
- Be careful! Sometimes the bully victim will laugh to play along—but usually you can tell if a person is in distress or faking the laughter.

Definition of Cyberbullying

- "*Cyberbullying* involves the use of information and communication technologies to support deliberate, repeated, and hostile behavior by an individual or group that is intended to harm others."
- Basically, it is bullying by use of technology.
- Facebook, MySpace, text messages, e-mails, sexting, YouTube (a recording of a fight or bullying of another student)
- Danger—it is even more secretive and hard to recognize than standard bullying. (Tell the teachers you will discuss the dangers of bullying later in the workshop.)

Effects of Being Bullied

- Lack of trust
- Substance abuse
- Anxiety/panic attacks
- Isolation—lack of relationships
- Eating disorders
- Depression
- Possible violence/aggression toward others (for example, Columbine)
- *Suicide!!* This is an epidemic!

Suicide and Bullying

- Recent research shows that students who are bullied between sixth and 10th grade are at a 50 percent higher risk for attempting suicide than students who are not bullied (or not bullied for a long period of time).
- There is hope. . . . If we stop bullying now, we can help save a life!!

Signs a Student Is Being Bullied

- Withdrawal
- Depression
- Sitting alone or not hanging with friends
- Refusing to go to lunch

- Lagging behind in class when the bell rings
- Asking to go to the nurse because of frequent headaches or not feeling well
- Increasing absenteeism
- Not wanting to participate in physical education or group activities
- Changing their appearance/dress
- Not participating in class/raising hand
- Asking teacher to move their seat
- Offering to help the teacher during lunch or recess
- Showing an overall change in behavior

"If you are concerned about a student, just *ask!* Maybe you will be wrong, but better safe than sorry!!!"

Teachers can create a safe and bully-free classroom if they know how to recognize bullying and the signs that a student is being bullied!

"*Say* and *do* something *immediately!* Bullying only exists because people ignore it! Bullying thrives on silence!"

How Do We Talk to Students about Bullying?

- Small groups by grade level
- Maybe gender-specific groups—up to the teacher
- If there is evidence of "cliques" or bullying in the class, it is best to break up class/groups.
- Students are much more vulnerable when they are alone and not with their friends or "cliques."
- Power in numbers—bullies have power because they usually have followers who are too afraid to speak up themselves.
- Get the class comfortable with an exercise or opening activity.

Sample Opening Exercises/Activities

Explain the following activities to the teachers:

Strength Exercise

- This can be done to create class cohesiveness before you begin talking about bullying.
- Hand out blank index cards. Instruct the students to write "Strength" on one side. On the other side, tell the students to write about a time they used a strength to overcome an obstacle.

- *Note:* Make sure you explain what a strength is before the exercise. Tell the students that it is a characteristic of their personality or something they are good at, not always physical strength.
- Some examples: being a good listener, being good at sports, getting good grades, being able to make friends easily, and so on.
- Have the class share with each other when they wrote.

Red Zone Exercise

- Teacher leads the activity/discussion.
- Ask the students to make a list of places in the school where bullying is more likely to occur. Make a list of these on the board.
- Examples: gym locker room, hallways, buses, the playground, and so on.
- Tell the students that these areas are now going to be called the "red zone" areas. Notify teachers, administrators, and other students about these areas so that more staff can be placed at these areas. Also, encourage the students to say the words "red zone area" when they witness a student being bullied in one of them.

"Similar" or "In Common" Exercise

- Research shows that students are less likely to bully or pick on kids they feel they have something in common with.
- Tell the students to get into groups of three to five (depending on if this is done in a large or small group).
- Tell them to write down as many things as possible that they *all* have in common. Examples: favorite food, favorite TV show, all live in the same state, all have pets, and so on.
- Ask the students to write down things that are difficult, not just easy things.
- Make each student speak to every other student in the group.
- Allow the students three to five minutes to complete the list.

Tell the teachers that these activities are sample ice breakers and should precede a discussion about bullying.

Activity

Break the teachers up into pairs, or ask them to break themselves up into groups of two or three.

Tell them they will be doing an activity involving communication with parents and students about bullying.

Hand out the scenarios to each group. Several groups will have the same scenarios. Break the teachers into parent and kid pairs or groups of three.

Ask the teachers to create a dialogue of how they would deal with their given scenario. They will share and role play to the class. Tell them, "Be creative! Act it out! Pretend it is real! How would the kid or parent act?"

Scenarios:

1. A parent has come in for a meeting to talk with you about her son Johnny, who is 12 years old and in seventh grade. He has been complaining about being picked on in your class, is now afraid to come to school, and has stayed home the past few days pretending to be sick.

2. Susie, a 14-year-old girl, has asked to speak to you privately. She has come to you and told you that her friends who she has been friends with since kindergarten no longer want to be friends with her, and she is really upset about it. She feels she is all alone and tells you she has been crying every night. She has not told her parents about any of this.

3. You have noticed that lately Lila, a 13-year-old girl, has become withdrawn and less talkative in class. She has been requesting to come to your room during lunchtime, and you've noticed that she has been walking alone in the hallways and is always by herself. You suspect she may be being bullied. She is coming to your room today for lunch, and you want to try and find out what is wrong with her. (Through your discussion with Lila, you find out there is an older girl bullying her.)

4. Joey, a 17-year-old athlete who is very popular in the school, has been called to your attention by the principal for bullying kids in your class. You were honestly unaware that this was happening. However, your principal wants you to speak with Joey about his behavior in class and put a stop to it immediately.

Have one group for each scenario present to the class.

Ask the teachers, "What did you think was good? What wasn't so good? Was this task difficult? Was it easy? What did you like or not like about the scenarios presented?" Continue your presentation after the activity is done.

What Do We Do about Bullying?

Teachers Don't

- Blame the victim.
- Say it's the victim's fault.

- Tell the victim to ignore it.
- Participate in bullying or making fun of other kids—even if it is funny (you are the students' role model).
- Make inappropriate jokes.
- Allow cell phones in class.
- Keep silent—this helps bullies! Remember bullying thrives on silence!
- Fight back.
- Bully the bully or make fun of them in class.
- Ignore it or encourage students to ignore it.

Teachers Do

- Listen to the student who has been bullied.
- Support the victim.
- Encourage students to come to you about bullying or if they are having a problem with a peer—especially if it's in your class.
- Make a referral to the social worker/guidance counselor if necessary.
- Talk to the student who is bullying others (they need help too!).
- Get to know your students.
- Pay attention to changes in student behavior.
- Create a safe classroom by setting guidelines from the first day—keep reminding students about these guidelines.
- *Talk about it! Constantly!*
- Recognize and remain aware of your own insecurities and biases about bullying.
- If you are uncomfortable or don't know what to do or say, get help from the social worker or counselor, an administrator, or a peer teacher—but *do something!*
- Encourage parent–child communication (maybe talk about your bully-free classroom or no bullying policy at Meet the Teacher Night).
- Talk with parents about bullying. Explain what it is and what it isn't. Educate them.
- Tell your students not to participate in bullying by spreading rumors or ignoring bullying behavior.
- *Remember*: As long as bullying is kept a secret, it will continue! Bullies thrive on silence—it gives them power! Take the power away by standing up to it and encouraging your students to stand up to it by telling a trusted adult!!

Interventions

- Buddy system—creating a schoolwide buddy system, pairing younger students with older students

- Peer mediation
- Stopping it immediately
- Talking about it constantly—advisories, homerooms, or weekly or daily check-ins (this only takes two minutes per day)
- Knowing your students and watching for signs of bullying
- Taking the power away from the bully by not ignoring it
- Using "Red Zone," "In Common," and "Strength" exercises to increase class cohesiveness
- Reading from books about bullying and having a class discussion
- Talking about it so students become comfortable
- Talking and meeting with a student who is bullying others (possible referral to counselor/social worker)

"Implementing these interventions and strategies in your class will only take a little time away from teaching. Isn't it worth it to create a bully-free classroom and ensure the safety of your students? Honestly, who can learn when they are scared or being bullied?"

Recap with the teachers about the presentation. Tell them that you gave them a lot of information, and this should have provided them with an overview of how to begin dealing with bullying in their classroom.

Remind the teachers that the *only* way to combat bullying is for the *entire* school to work together and develop appropriate prevention and intervention strategies to combat it.

Encourage teachers to speak with you privately if they have further questions or concerns.

BEHAVIOR MANAGEMENT/TEACHER–STUDENT RELATIONSHIP PROFESSIONAL DEVELOPMENT

Materials: Paper, pens, dry erase/chalk board, "Tips For Teachers Working with Difficult Students"

Time: 45 minutes

Introduce the topic of professional development to the teachers: behavior management for students by forming relationships.

Begin by saying, "[School Name] is all about student relationships. Do your lesson plans, make sure you have a code of conduct set up in your classroom, go to lunch and hall duty, but most importantly—*form relationships* with your students. We *need* to arm students for the real world. Plus, if you take time to form relationships with students in the beginning of the school year, your discipline problems should decrease."

Say to the group, "So, how do you form relationships with *all* of your students? You may think that this is impossible to do. You may say to me that you have five classes of 25 students per day, hall duty, lunch duty, an elective class, and only one prep period a day, making it impossible to take the time to form relationships with your students.

"I am not insinuating that you are not extremely busy and hardworking individuals; I am only offering some tips and advice on how to help manage some of your difficult students."

Activity

Hand out paper and pens to the teachers. Instruct them to write down a few things that prevent them from forming relationships with *each* and *every* student they serve. Ask them to include some things like which students are difficult to form relationships with and so on. Give examples, including not enough time in the day, an angry student, a student who is absent a lot, and so on. Allow two to three minutes for this activity.

After the teachers are done writing, ask for volunteers to share their answers. You will record the answers on a chart on the dry erase or chalk board titled "Barriers to Forming Relationships with Students."

After you have compiled a long list of barriers, ask the teachers to reflect as a group about the list. What do they think of the list? Is there anything they can do as individuals to change some of the barriers on the list? Is there anything the school can do to change some of the barriers on the list?

Allow 10 minutes or so for the discussion, but be careful to not let it morph into a complaint session. This is about helping the teachers, not criticizing them.

Tell the teachers you are going to offer some tips on how to form relationships with students:

- Stand at your classroom door and greet each student with a handshake and by name *every day*.
- Get to know your students by asking them questions. Example: "Joey, I see you are carrying an instrument, do you play?"

- Allow two to five minutes in the beginning of your class for a group-building or check-in activity. Check-ins could be just a simple "How is everyone doing today? Does anyone have anything to share about their weekend [or week]? Did anyone see any good movies? Did anyone have a difficult week that they would like to talk about?" (Activities from this book could be photocopied and handed out to teachers who are interested.)
- Give pats on the back and smiles. Encourage your students. Show them you are a person too and are interested in them, not just in teaching them a curriculum.
- Show an interest in your students. When they giggle, ask them what is funny. Ask them what their favorite color is. Try and get to know each student a little more each day. (This can be done individually or as a group.)

Be Aware

Say to the teachers, "Know thyself.

"Which students are you avoiding? Why? Are you afraid of them? Do they tick you off? What feelings are they instilling in you? Can you *still* make sure that you are treating *every* student equally and giving *every* student an *equal* opportunity to succeed at [School Name]? If not, maybe you should seek out a peer teacher or the social worker for guidance. It is not easy to form relationships with *every* student. It is very difficult, especially with students who are hard to manage. You may not be successful forming relationships with *each* and *every* student, but you need to try and keep trying. Do not give up!

"Self-reflect: Continue to ask yourself three questions pertaining to forming relationships with your students, throughout the school year. These three questions should especially be asked if you find yourself with an extremely challenging student:

"What am I doing that is working?

"What am I doing that doesn't seem to be working?

"Do I have relationships with *all* my students? Why or why not?"

Say to the teachers, "The idea is that if [School Name] students feel they have relationships with *all* teachers they come across, they will be armed to go out in the real world. We are these students' 'parents' for seven hours each day. How can we ensure that we are being good role models and arming these students with the tools they need to be successful in this harsh world? Forming relationships with students models for them the fact that relationships are a necessary and important part of life. The more difficult a student is, the harder it is and the *more* important it is to form a relationship with them. More often than not, a difficult student has had difficulties forming relationships in the past. Perhaps they come from a difficult home situation or have an abusive past. Some children just have trouble trusting others. Whatever the reason, forming relationships with *all* students is important.

"By giving these students a chance and taking the time to get to know them and be there for them, we are showing them that we *do* care and we *do* believe in them. We are arming them with self-confidence and hope for a successful and promising future.

"Again, I am not saying it will be easy or possible to form relationships with *each and every* student. I am simply asking you to try and to keep trying. You may surprise yourself. Just a simple 'Hello, how are you?' to each student can make a world of a difference in their lives."

Pass out the "Tips for Teachers Working with Difficult Students" (see p. 140) and explain that this will help the teachers in working with difficult students in their classrooms.

Thank the teachers for coming to the professional development workshop, and let them know that you are available to them if they have further questions or concerns. Dismiss the teachers.

PEER MEDIATION PROFESSIONAL DEVELOPMENT

Materials: None

Time: 20 to 25 minutes

This professional development is to be conducted in conjunction with starting a peer mediation program at your school. (Training for and implementation of the peer mediation program is discussed thoroughly in chapter 4 ["Workshops and School Programs"].) This professional development training is meant as an introduction to the program for teachers.

Note: This training should be conducted when the peer mediation program is about to begin. In other words, you should have already discussed the program with your administrator, secured a room, and so on. Please refer to chapter 3 ("Group Implementation and Counseling Activities") for further clarification.

Peer Mediation: Students Helping Students

What Is It?

- Peer mediation is a type of conflict resolution. It is a way for students to deal with differences without coercion.

TIPS FOR TEACHERS WORKING WITH DIFFICULT STUDENTS

- Set guidelines/rules: Be clear in what you want the student to do.

- Establish clear consequences: State clearly what the consequences will be if the student breaks a rule or class guideline.

- Be consistent: Follow your guidelines and consequences *every* time!

- Reward positive behaviors: When the student is behaving appropriately, reward them with praise, awards, privileges, or prizes.

- Ignore negative behaviors: Do *not* give attention to the difficult student when they are engaging in a negative activity.

- Create a behavior chart or behavior plan: State the consequences and rewards for appropriate and inappropriate behavior.

- Get the student involved! Have the student be involved in creating and coming up with rewards for positive behaviors and consequences for negative behaviors.

- Give leadership roles to students who are disruptive because of lack of focus.

- Talk to the student one-on-one. (Students are often embarrassed to be singled out in class. Make time to talk to the student before or after class, when other students are not around.)

- Form a relationship with the student: Take the time to get to know the student. This will decrease the negative behaviors.

- *Never take it personally!!* This will make you react out of emotion rather than being proactive.

- Forgive the student: Start each day fresh. If the student committed an infraction on Wednesday, when they come into school on Thursday, start fresh. Verbalize this to the student so that they feel they are starting with a clean slate.

TIPS FOR TEACHERS WORKING WITH DIFFICULT STUDENTS (CONTINUED)

- Do *not* engage in a power struggle with the student: If the student is being argumentative, simply say, "Johnny, I see that you are upset, and I would like to discuss this with you at a later time, but I can't right now because I need to get through the reading lesson. Please give me the respect to finish the lesson, and I promise to speak with you after class." Then move on. If the student persists, repeat the statement. Make sure you *do* meet with Johnny after class.

- Do *not* raise your voice with or yell at the student.

- Develop a code word or nonverbal cue between you and the difficult student that signals they are having a difficult time or need a break or "time out."

- Do speak in a calm and regular tone when disciplining a student. Yelling or raising your voice will only cause the student to become defensive and engage in a power struggle.

- Do ask the student what is causing their inappropriate behavior in your class. The student may be able to provide insight into their behavior that you have not thought of.

- Smile and show the student you care about them *every day!* (This is difficult but *so* important.)

- Do not bully or instigate power struggles with the student.

- Do recognize the student's need for your attention.

- Pat yourself on the back for trying even when you are at your wit's end.

- Do celebrate yourself for being a good and effective teacher!

- It works to resolve conflicts in schools, because through it students gain power and responsibility.
- It is a step-by-step process that ultimately leads to an agreement between disputing parties.

Goals of Peer Mediation

- To enable students to take responsibility for peacefully resolving disputes without the intervention of staff
- To increase the ability of students to deal effectively with issues of cultural and social diversity
- To prevent disputes from escalating into incidents that require disciplinary action
- To create a school climate that is safe and focused on collaboration and cooperation

When Do We Use It?

We use peer mediation when two or more students cannot reach an agreement.

Examples:

- Students caught fighting
- Students arguing or about to fight
- Friends who are now arguing or not speaking to each other
- Bullying incidents—sometimes. It depends on whether the victim of bullying wants to mediate with the bully. Never force mediation! Mediation is voluntary!
- Copying/plagiarism incidents
- Rumor incidents
- Basically, any conflict between two or more students!

How Does It Work?

- Peer mediators will fill out an application and go through a selection process, meeting all requirements. (State the requirements you came up with when reading about how to begin and implement a peer mediation program in your school.)
- All peer mediators will attend and complete an eight-week training led by the school social worker.

Peer Mediator Selection Process (Example)

Students *must* meet all requirements:

- Must be in 11th or 12th grade (this can be modified to fit your school)
- Must not have any recent disciplinary referrals
- Must be in good academic standing (passing all classes)
- Must complete an application and obtain two teacher signatures/recommendation letters
- May have to complete an interview with the school social worker

Peer Mediator Application

Pass out a sample "Peer Mediator Application" (see p. 97) to the teachers to show them what the application looks like. Tell them they that may be approached by a student requesting a signature. They are allowed to sign more than one application, but they should only sign for students they believe will make effective peer mediators.

Training of Peer Mediators

- "I am going to conduct an intensive eight-week training session on peer mediation.
- "The training will include active listening skills, antibullying procedures, how to remain impartial, diversity, how to write an agreement, and so on.
- "After training is completed, mediators will be required to meet with me weekly or biweekly to continue perfecting their skills."

Referrals to Peer Mediation

- When two or more students are fighting, cheating, copying, or bullying, they should be referred to the administration as part of the school's code of conduct. Administration will then determine whether they should go to peer mediation.
- When two or more students are in conflict but have not committed a major infraction, they may be referred to peer mediation by a teacher or staff member
- A student can request mediation on their own.

Students *must* agree to mediate. They don't have to volunteer, but they *must* agree to take part in the mediation.

How Do I Request Peer Mediations?

Pass out copies of the "Peer Mediation Request Form" (see p. 118) for teachers to keep.

- Pick up a request/referral form from the school social worker.
- Fill it out and return it to school social worker's office.

Putting It All Together

Implementation of peer mediation:

- Student selection process
- Students complete training
- Referrals begin (pick up requests from the school social worker's office)
- School social worker assigns mediator to conduct mediation
- Mediation occurs
- Peer mediators will have set times that they are available for mediation.
- Social worker will be available at these times as well.
- Mediation is over when an agreement is reached.

Promoting the Program

- Peer mediators will make flyers/posters and put them around the school.
- After training, peer mediators will come into homerooms and promote the program.
- Brochures will be available for students and teachers. (Pass out sample pamphlet for teachers to look at [see pp. 121–122].)

Why Peer Mediation?

- Statistics show that schools that have peer mediation programs have less violence than do other schools (Schrumpf et al., 1997a, 1997b).
- Peer mediation creates a safe and open-minded culture.
- Peer mediation teaches students how to handle conflicts in healthy ways.
- Peer mediation teaches students of different backgrounds to work together.
- Peer mediation offers an alternative to traditional disciplinary interventions.

Ask the teachers if they have questions. Tell them that the program is in start-up mode and that it will take a little time to implement it. Encourage them to share their thoughts and concerns about the program. Dismiss the teachers.

TIPS FOR WORKING WITH STUDENTS WITH AUTISM SPECTRUM DISORDERS

- Students with autism spectrum disorders (ASDs) are visual learners.

    Tip: Write out directions for these students, rather than giving verbal directions.

- Show students with ASDs how to complete an assignment by giving them an example.

    Tip: Remember to make the example visual. Often, students with ASDs can't even comprehend verbal directions.

    Tip: Combine pictures with written directions.

- *Eye Contact:* Students with ASDs have actually reported that it is painful to look someone in the eye.

    Tip: Tell the students to focus on your nose or forehead rather than looking you in the eye. Don't interpret their lack of eye contact as rudeness or shyness.

- *Social Skills:* Students with ASDs often lack social skills.

    Tip: Do not force them to work with other students; rather, encourage them to work with other students on their own time. If they want to work alone, allow them to do so.

- *Communication:* Students with ASDs have difficulty understanding and empathizing with others. For example, if you say to a student that your aunt died, rather than the normal response of "I'm sorry," a student with an ASD may ask "Why did she die?" or "How did she die?" Students with ASDs have extreme difficulty putting themselves in others' shoes. If they see teasing or another student laughing, they may automatically assume it is about them.

    Tip: Tell the student with an ASD that there is no reason to think or evidence to suggest that the other person is laughing at them or making fun of them.

    Tip: Repeat directions several times in the same voice. This helps the student with an ASD remember the directions. Giving directions only once makes it difficult for them to understand or remember them.

    Tip: Speak clearly and slowly to students with ASDs. Give directions one at a time. Example: "John, please do questions 1 through 5." This is better than "John, do questions 1 through 5 and then turn your paper in and then open up your book and begin the next lesson." That is too overwhelming and confusing for students with ASDs.

TIPS FOR WORKING WITH STUDENTS WITH AUTISM SPECTRUM DISORDERS (CONTINUED)

- *Anxiety:* Students with ASDs tend to become overly anxious at times.

    Tip: If you see signs of anxiety or nervousness, go directly to the student and offer positive encouragement. Say, "You can do this. Calm down—there is no reason to get upset. Just do each problem one at a time."

- Students with ASDs do much better when directly interacted with and given directions to rather than when the directions are given to the class as a whole.

    Tip: Give the entire class the directions, and then approach the student with an ASD and give them the directions separately.

- *Organization:* This can be a challenge for students with ASDs.

    Tip: Make planners, checklists, special homework sheets, and reminder lists for students with ASDs. Again, remember that they are visual learners.

- Students with ASDs have difficulty completing big projects from start to finish.

    Tip: Make sequentially numbered steps for the student so they know what to do as they progress toward completion of the project. Use task analysis or chunk directions/assignments.

- Students with ASDs usually respond to positive reinforcement and rewards.

    Tip: Offer immediate rewards or praise directly after the student exhibits positive behavior or completes a task. Example, "Good job, Joey, for completing question 1. Now move on to question 2, please."

PROBLEMS COMMON AMONG STUDENTS WITH AUTISM SPECTRUM DISORDERS

- Writing is extremely challenging for students with autism spectrum disorders (ASDs), especially creative writing. Students with ASDs have difficulty with creativity. Example: A normally developing child may pick up a stick and pretend it is a sword or a gun. A student with an ASD sees a stick as a stick.

    Tip: Offer the student ideas of creativity, rather than just asking them to come up with an idea on their own.

- Organization is very difficult for students with ASDs.

- Students with ASDs struggle with sensorimotor skills. Sounds can be very bothersome and distracting. Bothersome sounds can range from a loud fire alarm to the simple scratching of a pencil on paper.

- Students with ASDs often feel overstimulated in certain environments. It can help to have the student sit up front in the class and or to remove some of the excessive visual stimulation around the student. (Too many colorful posters in the classroom may be distracting or overstimulating.)

- *Coordination Problems:* Students with ASDs have difficulty in physical education class because they have difficulty with sensorimotor skills. For example, imagine feeling like you are driving a car, and when you want to turn right, the car actually goes left. Students with ASDs want their bodies to move in certain ways but are unable to make that connection between their brain and body.

Keep these issues in mind when working with a student with an ASD.

Chapter 6

COMMUNICATING WITH PARENTS

This chapter covers communication between parents and school social workers. Examples of effective communication are described in detail, including issues such as talking with a parent about a difficult student, a student who is being bullied, and a student who is bullying others. In addition, how to talk to a parent about a student who is suicidal or engaging in self-harming behaviors is addressed.

When communicating with parents, it is a good idea to keep the following guidelines in mind: show empathy, show support, and remain nonjudgmental. Effective communication with parents is similar to effective communication with teachers, as covered in chapter 5. Parents, like teachers, can be defensive around or wary of school social workers. Some parents think that if their child has to see the social worker, something is wrong with their child, which may mean they did something wrong as parents. Parents from some cultures view asking for or receiving help as a weakness and, therefore, do not want social work intervention. Other parents may be afraid that their child will be classified and receive special education services if referred for social work services. Many parents, however, value school social workers and often reach out to get services for their child. Regardless, communication with *all* parents should be effective.

As mentioned in chapter 5, effective communication is all about the approach. How you choose to approach communication will either open or close the dialogue. This is also true when communicating with parents. If you approach a parent showing empathy, support, and nonjudgment, the parent is much more likely to want to hear what you have to offer. As noted regarding teachers in chapter 5, active listening is an important part of communicating with parents as well. Listen to parents' concerns before offering interventions. Convey that you are there to help their child and *not* to criticize or judge their parenting. When working with parents, I like to use the strength-based approach (Epstein, 2000), whereby you begin the conversation by stating a strength about the student before delving into the areas that need improvement. For example, if Johnny's parents are coming in for a meeting about Johnny failing every class, you could start the discussion with "Johnny is a very funny young man. He makes me laugh all the time." Then you could move into a discussion about Johnny's failing his classes. The strength-based approach lightens the air a bit and makes the parents feel more comfortable from the beginning of the meeting. Examples of how to communicate effectively with parents on various subjects are provided here.

HOW TO TALK TO PARENTS ABOUT A DIFFICULT STUDENT

Communicating to parents that their child is failing or having difficulties in school is never an easy task. No parent wants to hear that their child is not being successful. In this situation, parents may feel defensive or responsible for their child's behavior. They may be resistant to help or believe that you are going to judge and criticize them. To best help the parents and the student, you want to convey an empathic, supportive, and nonjudgmental attitude from the beginning of the discussion. Ideally, a face-to-face meeting between parents and social worker is best, but that is not always possible. A sample of how to talk to parents about a difficult student is provided here.

Social Worker: Hi, Mr. and Mrs. Smith. My name is _____, and I'm the school social worker at _____ School. Thank you for coming to meet with me to discuss Johnny's behavior. I want you to know that I'm not here to judge or criticize you in any way. I'm here to offer my support and services to you in an effort to help ensure Johnny's success here.

Mrs. Smith: Okay, I understand. Thank you for inviting us to come in. We know Johnny is very difficult to deal with. In fact, he has always been a troubled child. We used to get called into his last school quite frequently. We are used to his behavior problems.

Social Worker: It sounds like you have heard a lot of negative things about Johnny's behavior through the years. I can imagine it must be difficult to get called into the school for a meeting about your son's behavior.

Mrs. Smith: Yes it is.

Social Worker: First off I want to tell you how much I have enjoyed working with Johnny. He is a real character. He is so creative. Sometimes he shows me his drawings of cartoon characters. Your son has talent for sure.

Mr. Smith (chuckling): Thank you.

Social Worker: The reason I've asked you to come in to meet with me today is that it has come to my attention that Johnny is disruptive in his classes and the hallways. Teachers have told me that Johnny talks out of turn, doesn't complete his homework, and was recently involved in a physical altercation with another student.

Mr. Smith (nodding): Uh huh.

Social Worker: I know this may be difficult to hear about your son, but, again, remember that we are all here to learn how to help Johnny be successful.

Mrs. Smith: Okay.

Social Worker: As Johnny's parents, you know him better than anyone. Can you think of a reason that may be causing him to act out in school? Perhaps you can help us help him by telling me a little more about how Johnny is at home.

Mrs. Smith: Well, Johnny has always had problems in school. He can't focus or sit still. He never does his homework and often reacts quickly. He has a younger sister, and he is always fighting with her. We just don't know what to do with him. We have tried our best, but it doesn't seem to help. We love him so much but just can't get him to behave.

Social Worker: Johnny is lucky to have such caring parents.

Mr. and Mrs. Smith: Thank you.

Social Worker: You mentioned that Johnny has trouble sitting still and completing his homework. Does he get easily distracted?

Mrs. Smith: Oh yes. I ask him a question, and he gets so distracted and forgets even what I asked him after 30 seconds! I have to ask him to do his homework five times before he even sits down to do it!

Social Worker: This concerns me. When did Johnny start having difficulties with focusing?

Mrs. Smith: Hmm, I think as long as I can remember, but it got worse as he got into the higher grades.

Social Worker: Mr. and Mrs. Smith, although I am not a diagnostician, it sounds like Johnny may have trouble focusing and staying on task due to his inability to sustain attention for long periods of time. Would you consider taking Johnny to his pediatrician for an evaluation?

Mr. Smith: What kind of evaluation? What would this mean for Johnny? Would he have to be on medication?

Social Worker: It depends on what the pediatrician determines. However, Johnny may have trouble focusing in school due to his inability to sustain attention, and if untreated, it may get worse as he gets older and moves on to higher grades where the work is more demanding. This could explain why he gets easily agitated and reacts aggressively to others, as you mentioned he does with his sister.

Mrs. Smith: I guess it would be a good idea to take him to the pediatrician and find out if there is something wrong with him.

Social Worker: I think that is a good place to start. In the meantime, what can I do for Johnny in school to help him be successful?

Mr. Smith: I don't know. I just want him to get good grades and behave in class!

Social Worker: I have an idea. What if we all met with Johnny and his teachers and created a behavior plan? The plan would include a list of positive behaviors that Johnny would be expected to display. Then, when he displayed them, he would receive a reward or privilege. What do you think about that idea?

Mr. Smith: I love it! Can we do that for Johnny at home too?!

Social Worker: Absolutely. In fact, I think it is important that we continue to communicate frequently so we can follow Johnny's progress with the behavior plan. I can report back to you on his progress at school, and you can report back to me on his progress at home.

Mrs. Smith: I like that idea. Call anytime.

Social Worker: I think we make a good team! So, just to recap, our plan is that you will take Johnny to the pediatrician for an evaluation. A behavior plan will be set up for Johnny in school, and we will have ongoing communication to monitor Johnny's progress. Does that sound right?

Mrs. Smith: Yes, that sounds good, and we agree. Thank you so much.

Social Worker: It was my pleasure. I look forward to working with you and Johnny to ensure his academic and emotional success at _____ School.

This example covers a range of effective communication techniques. Empathy and support are conveyed straight from the beginning in the social worker's introduction. The strength-based approach is used when the social worker acknowledges Johnny's creativity. A nonjudgmental attitude is offered through the social worker's active listening throughout the discussion. The social worker listens to the parents *first* and *then* offers suggestions for intervention. Only after gaining the parents' cooperation does the social worker make suggestions. Acknowledging that the meeting may be difficult for the parents is a way of joining with them. Validating the parents for their efforts is also a way to join them. You may notice that the social worker asks the parents for feedback on suggestions instead of telling them what to do. Remember, you and the parents want to work together as a team. This will be the best way to help a student to be successful.

Note: Although this example is obviously of a student who displays symptoms of attention-deficit disorder (ADD) or attention-deficit/hyperactivity disorder (ADHD), it is usually a good idea to leave diagnosis to a medical doctor or psychologist. You may have the appropriate license to be able to diagnose, but remember that you are a school professional and diagnosing is not your main priority. In fact, in some states, school social workers are not seen as diagnosticians and are not allowed to diagnose. In addition, parents may not be ready to hear a diagnosis, so leaving the name of any possible condition out is recommended. It is fine to mention symptoms of ADD or ADHD, but always preface it with "I am not a diagnostician or medical doctor. But . . ." My advice is to be careful with diagnosing students in schools and sharing it with parents. Leave diagnosis to the school psychologist or a pediatrician.

You should notice that before the meeting ended, the social worker recapped and stated the "plan of action," or intervention. I have seen many meetings that have lasted for hours and never arrived at a conclusive plan of action. It is important to go into the meeting with a plan, but it's more important to *leave* with a plan. As a social worker, you may have ideas of what you want to do with a child even before you meet with their parents. This is okay, because it guides you in facilitating the meeting. However, I caution you not to be close-minded. You need to view yourself and the parents of the child as a team. The parents may come up with some great suggestions or offer you new information that will alter your original plan of action. When ending the meeting, always recap the plan of action. This sums up the meeting and provides good closure for both the parents and you. In addition, it holds the parents and you accountable for each of your parts in the plan of action. It is imperative that social workers work with parents. Sometimes just including the parents in their child's education is all that is needed to help the child be successful. You, as a social worker, can ask parents to implement interventions at home that are used in school, as stated in the example about a behavior plan. Even when working with the most resistant and hard-to-reach parents, I have never met a parent that truly didn't want to help their child be successful.

Ongoing communication between the social worker and parents is essential to ensuring the success of any student who is struggling at school.

TIP: Call parents of students with behavior problems with good news, *not* only with bad news. So many times, parents only receive calls from schools when their child is in trouble. I can't tell you how many times I have called a parent with good news about their child's behavior, and the answer I receive on the other end is filled with hesitation. I actually had a parent tell me that they were afraid to pick up the phone when they saw the school's number. Don't let this happen to you. Call with good news too. Would you want to only hear bad news about your child? How about if every time you came into school each morning, your principal called you into their office to berate you and tell you what a bad job you were doing? You would start avoiding your principal and maybe even enter through the school's back door! This is how it feels to parents who only get negative feedback about their child.

After I started calling a father with good news about a child who was always getting in trouble, he thanked me and told me he had never received a phone call with good news from his daughter's school. You can also get creative when a student does well and, in addition to calling home with a good report, send a little note home to the parents, use Publisher to create a "Most Improved" certificate, and so on. Too much of discipline in schools is focused on what students do *wrong*. Try to focus on what they do *right*, and then reward that. You will see a huge change in behavior as well as an increase in parental involvement.

HOW TO TALK TO PARENTS ABOUT A STUDENT WHO IS BEING BULLIED

Bullying is an extremely sensitive topic in schools these days. Students are committing acts of violence, such as school shootings and killing themselves, due to being bullied. Bullying is *not* a light issue and should be viewed with the same sensitivity as the issue of suicide. This section covers how to talk to a parent about a student who is being bullied. For the purpose of this exercise, the example includes a discussion with parents who are not aware that their child is a victim of bullying.

Social Worker: Thank you for coming to meet with me, Mr. and Mrs. Smith. I would like to discuss a concern that has been brought to my attention regarding your daughter, Cindy. Cindy is aware that I will be speaking with you and has agreed for me to break confidentiality regarding what I am about to tell you. Cindy revealed to me in a counseling session that she is being bullied by a female classmate of hers.

Mr. Smith: What? Bullied? What happened? I'm gonna kill this other girl! How dare anyone hurt our daughter?!

Social Worker (maintaining a calm tone): I can imagine how difficult this news must be for you. However, the best way for us to help Cindy is to remain calm so that we can decide the best plan of action to help your daughter.

Mrs. Smith (crying): I understand. It's just so upsetting! We've never wanted our poor little girl to get hurt. Why didn't she say anything to us?

Social Worker: Many times children who are bullied feel shame and blame themselves. Don't blame yourself for Cindy not coming to you. It was probably extremely difficult for Cindy to even talk about the incident at all. In fact, Cindy didn't use the word "bullied" when she told me about this other girl. It was me who told her that the behavior she was describing was bullying. Cindy is very afraid of what the other girl will do now that she has told. I assured Cindy that what she told me would remain confidential from the other student but that it was imperative that I speak with you and discuss this matter with the principal. Bullying is a serious matter, and I assure you that _____ School takes all cases of bullying very seriously.

Mrs. Smith: Thank you. We want to make sure this never happens again. Who is the girl that is bullying our daughter, and what did she do?

Social Worker: I cannot reveal the name of the other student as she has a right to privacy as mandated by education laws. However, I can assure you that the school will be taking this matter very seriously and that the other student will be given appropriate consequences. If Cindy decides to tell you the identity of the other girl, that is up to her. As far as what the other girl did, Cindy said that she has been shoving her in the halls, spreading rumors about her, and laughing and pointing at Cindy when she walks by.

Mr. Smith: Shoving her? Oh my gosh! This is unacceptable—I want to press charges!

Social Worker: It is your absolute right if you feel you would like to involve the police in this matter. As a school, we will cooperate fully with the authorities and share any information that we have. However, I must advise you that sometimes involving the authorities can be very traumatic for everyone involved, especially a child who is being bullied, like Cindy.

Mr. Smith: Yes, I can see what you mean. So, how is Cindy now? What is the school going to do?

Social Worker: Cindy seemed to feel better after telling me about this other student. I told her it was the right thing to do, that no one should keep bullying to themselves, nor should they have to endure what Cindy has been enduring. The school will take appropriate actions to ensure the safety of Cindy and of all the students. If classes need to be changed, we will do that, with your permission. I will also notify all of Cindy's teachers and all hall monitors about the situation so that they will be on alert. Additionally, necessary disciplinary consequences may be given to the student who is bullying Cindy. Counseling and other services will be offered to both Cindy and the other student. I want to work with you to develop a plan to help Cindy feel comfortable and safe here. No student should feel unsafe at school.

Mrs. Smith: Okay, it sounds like you take this matter seriously. I trust that you'll do what is best for our daughter. Change her classes if need be, or maybe it would be better to change the bully's classes. I don't know.

Social Worker: I haven't discussed with Cindy yet what she would like to do. She may want to stay in her classes, or she may want to switch. Either way, we will make sure that we act according to what she wants in order to make her feel safe and comfortable at school. I also encouraged Cindy to continue to talk to me about the situation so that I can help her through this difficult time as well as monitor any continued bullying. Many times I don't know about bullying because it is not revealed to me. Cindy did a brave thing by coming to me. You should be very proud of her.

Mrs. Smith: Oh, we are! Cindy is such a good girl. I just can't believe this happened to her. Can you ensure this won't happen again?

Social Worker: We are going to do everything in our power to ensure Cindy's safety at this school. We will put the necessary supports in place and, with Cindy's continued communication about any further bullying, we will be able to monitor it closely.

Mrs. Smith: Okay, that sounds good. What should we do?

Social Worker: My suggestion for you is to tell Cindy how proud you are of her and that she did the right thing by reporting the bullying. Encourage her to continue talking about what happened. Support her and tell her you love her.

Mrs. Smith (crying): We just want to help her through this.

Social Worker: You are already helping by working with the school to make sure this doesn't happen again. If you want, I can also offer you some referrals to an outside therapist if you feel Cindy would benefit from some additional counseling.

Mr. Smith: You think Cindy needs therapy? Is she that upset?

Social Worker: I am only making a suggestion that Cindy might benefit from therapy. Being a victim of bullying can be very detrimental to a child. Cindy's self-esteem may have suffered, and she may benefit from some additional form of counseling. If you do opt to go the therapy route, it may only be short-term counseling until Cindy feels better about the situation. Whatever you decide, I am here to help and answer any questions you may have. Please feel free to call me anytime.

Mr. Smith: Okay, thank you very much. We feel comfortable that our daughter is in such good hands. I think we will talk with Cindy first about therapy, and then if she wants it, we will call you for a referral. Is that okay?

Social Worker: Absolutely. Please call me with whatever you need. I am happy to help. I assure you that the school has Cindy's best interests at heart, and we will do everything necessary to ensure her safety at this school.

Mrs. Smith: Okay, thank you very much. Goodbye.

The example starts out with the social worker revealing the news about the child being bullied. The parents become upset and irate. The social worker acknowledges these feelings but then calms the parents down in an effort to get back to the issue at hand. Often in meetings about difficult issues, such as bullying, parents go on for a very long time about what the other student did. Although it is important that you allow time for parents to process their feelings regarding a situation, you want to make sure that you bring the meeting back to the topic at hand so that you can accomplish a plan of action. As previously mentioned, meetings should always have an agenda and end with a plan of action or intervention.

You may notice that throughout the example, the social worker repeats certain phrases, like "ensure her safety." This is done on purpose. The repetition makes it clear to the parents that the social worker is going to carry out what they say. It also gives the parents a sense of relief and comfort. You know the saying "you can never have too many compliments"? Well, it is the same idea when it comes to comforting and assuring parents about the safety of their child.

You may have also noticed that the confidentiality of the perpetrating student was upheld. This is an education law. You cannot reveal the name of the other student when speaking with parents. The parents may guess the name or already know the identity of the other student. That is fine, but you cannot reveal the name in the meeting.

The social worker is a bit vague when Mrs. Smith asks about what the school will do to protect Cindy. Ensuring the safety of all the students in the school should be the number one priority of the school. The social worker's answer remains vague because each school's policy regarding bullying is different. Ideally, before meeting with the parents, you will have met with your principal to determine the plan of action for ensuring the safety of the bullied student. There may be a specific school policy regarding incidents like these. You would then share this with the parents. However, not everything happens in an ideal way, and you may meet with the parents before you get a chance to meet with the principal to create a plan of action. This sort of dialogue helps the social worker in that case. My main point is that you just want to assure parents that the school will do everything necessary to protect the bullied student.

This example represents the first of probably many meetings with the parents of a bullied child. Bullying should not be ignored, and follow-up and monitoring of the situation is crucial.

HOW TO TALK TO PARENTS OF A STUDENT WHO IS BULLYING OTHER STUDENTS

When talking with parents about a child who is bullying others, you want to make sure that you use the same approach you use when talking with parents of a child who has been the victim of bullying. You want to offer your services to *all* students in need, not just victims. Often students who bully others have been bullied themselves. It is your job as the school social worker to intervene and provide effective strategies and interventions to stop the student from bullying others. At times, this may mean that an outside referral is necessary, especially if the student is showing aggression or being violent.

Parents most likely will become defensive after you tell them their child is bullying others. Be delicate in bringing this up and use the strength-based approach (Epstein, 2000). Convey that you want to help the student who is bullying others just as much as any students who are being bullied. This may be difficult for you as a social worker, because we all want to help victims. Helping perpetrators is another thing. It is important to hide your biases and judgments regarding the perpetrating student when working with their parents. If the parents feel that you don't like or want to help their child, they will become defensive and nothing will get accomplished. Remember to always keep your goal in mind: to ensure the academic and emotional success of *all* the students you serve.

Note: I am not advising you to ignore your biases or feelings about helping the perpetrating student. In fact, I would advise you to speak with your supervisor or another social worker regarding your feelings. I am, however, suggesting that you mask your negative feelings when working with the parents of a student who is bullying others. All students deserve compassion. A sample dialogue addressing this issue is provided here.

Social Worker: Good afternoon, Mr. and Mrs. Riley. Thank you for coming in to meet with me at such short notice. I want to discuss with you some concerns I have about your son, Charlie.

Mr. Riley (agitated and defensive): Yes, we were glad to come in. But we're confused. The principal called and told us that Charlie is being suspended for three days for fighting with another kid! What's going on? Charlie isn't the fighting type. We just want someone to explain what is going on and why Charlie has been suspended!

Social Worker: It sounds like you care a lot about Charlie. He is lucky to have such caring parents.

Mr. Riley: We do care very much about him. Thank you for saying that. Now, please tell us what happened.

Social Worker: Charlie was involved in a physical altercation today with a younger boy. After meeting with both boys and getting witness statements from students and teachers, my understanding is that Charlie was the one who started the fight.

Mrs. Riley (interrupting): What? That can't be. The other student must have hit him or done something to provoke him!

Social Worker: I know this must be difficult to hear, but it is also my understanding that Charlie has been bullying this other boy for several weeks now.

Mr. Riley: What?! How do you know this? Bullying? What is he doing?

Social Worker: I received my information from students, teachers, and witnesses to today's altercation. In addition, Charlie has confessed that he has been intentionally bothering this other boy.

Mr. Riley: Charlie said that?! Oh, he is gonna get it! He will be grounded for a month! This is *not* how we raised him!

Social Worker: I want you to know that Charlie's actions do not define him as a person. I believe Charlie has made some wrong decisions and that he needs help learning new ways to express his feelings. When I met with Charlie, he was very remorseful and apologized for hurting the other boy.

Mrs. Riley: I just don't understand why he is doing this. So, he hit the other boy?

Social Worker: According to the information I gathered and Charlie's statements, Charlie has been picking on this other boy by shoving him, calling him names, cornering him in the locker room, and then—today—punching him in the face.

Mrs. Riley: Oh my goodness! I can't believe Charlie would do such a thing! We are good parents! Where did we go wrong?

Social Worker: Mrs. Riley, please don't blame yourself. Bullying is very common in schools. It often occurs when students have low self-esteem, difficulty expressing their anger, or are seeking attention. However, it is a very serious matter, and the school takes bullying very seriously.

Mrs. Riley: I understand. So that is why Charlie is being suspended?

Social Worker: It is my understanding that Charlie was suspended due to the physical altercation today. However, further disciplinary action may be required because of Charlie's confession about bullying this other student. I would instruct you to meet with the principal with any further questions about discipline. I want to offer my services to both you and your husband and Charlie so that we can try and help him stop this behavior.

Mr. Riley: He can get counseling with you? We would like that.

Social Worker: Yes, I feel that meeting individually with Charlie to help him develop better ways to express his anger and feelings would be a good idea. However, I will also recommend some outside referrals for Charlie. Bullying behavior can be a sign of something else going on, and early treatment can make all the difference.

Mrs. Riley: Will Charlie be okay? Is he going to grow up to be a monster?

Social Worker: I am not saying that anything is wrong with Charlie. I am merely suggesting that Charlie might benefit from some additional services outside of school. I believe that Charlie is a nice young boy and has a bright future. I think he could benefit from some guidance and direction regarding his negative behaviors.

Mr. Riley: Well, don't you worry—we will hold Charlie accountable. He will not get away with this. This behavior is *not* tolerated in our family.

Social Worker: I do think that holding Charlie accountable for his actions will be good for him. Make sure you are consistent with your discipline and provide Charlie with an explanation of his punishment. In other words, tell Charlie that his behavior in school is not acceptable and, therefore, he will be grounded for a certain number of days, or whatever consequence you decide on.

Mrs. Riley: Thank you so much for meeting with us. We are so sorry that this happened and will definitely be talking to Charlie about it. We will ensure that this does *not* happen again. Please feel free to call us if anything like this ever happens again.

Social Worker: I appreciate you working with me. I think that if we continue to work together and monitor Charlie's behavior, we will be able to help him be successful at _____ School. Please feel free to call me as well with any questions or concerns that you may have.

The example starts out with an introduction and then uses the strength-based approach. In this example, the approach is used on the parents and not on the child. The reason for this is that the parents are quite defensive at the beginning of the meeting. The use of the strength-based approach helps calm them down and joins the social worker with them. Even though the parents start off in disbelief and denial, they eventually come around and are willing to work with the school social worker. Their defensiveness turns into anger at their son. Notice that the social worker explored the parents' feelings but also stated the facts about what Charlie did. The social worker remained objective and simply stated their knowledge of the situation, then offered services as well as appropriate referrals. You may also have noticed that effective discipline was covered. You want to make sure that you don't send extremely angry parents home to their child. I'm not saying that Charlie's parents would have abused Charlie or used excessive force, but you can't be sure. You want to make sure that parents process their thoughts and feelings with you before sending them home to their child. The plan of action in this intervention included the parents meeting with the school principal to address any further questions they had regarding Charlie's disciplinary consequences, the beginning and implementation of counseling with the school social worker and possible therapy outside of school, and how to effectively discipline Charlie at home.

HOW TO TALK TO PARENTS ABOUT A CHILD WHO IS SUICIDAL OR ENGAGING IN SELF-INJURIOUS BEHAVIORS

Protocol and suicide risk assessments are covered in chapter 7. The following communication provides you with an effective way to talk to parents about a child who is at risk for or is engaging in suicidal or self-injurious behaviors, such as cutting or self-mutilation. (For a detailed description of how to handle students with suicidal ideation, refer to chapter 7 ["Crisis Intervention—Protocol and Assessments"].)

Subjects such as suicide and self-mutilation should be dealt with by using the utmost compassion and empathy. Ultimately, you are telling parents that either their child is in danger of hurting themselves or is already engaging in these behaviors. You should expect strong emotional reactions from parents and be prepared to deal with the emotions that will be invoked in you. Of all the communication subjects I cover in this book, suicide and self-mutilation is by far the most difficult to discuss with a parent. An example of effective communication is provided here.

For the purpose of following through with the complete dialogue, we are going to assume that the child in the following example has been deemed a "low risk" by use of the assessment tool (provided in chapter 7) and does not need to be hospitalized.

Social Worker: Good afternoon, Mr. and Mrs. Kline. Thanks so much for coming in to meet with me regarding your daughter, Sarah.

Mrs. Kline: We came as soon as you called. We've never met with a school social worker before, and actually I'm a little worried about our daughter. Is Sarah okay?

Social Worker: What I am about to tell you may be very difficult for you to hear, but I want you to know that I am here to help both you and Sarah and that we will make a plan that will best serve Sarah's needs.

Mrs. Kline: Oh my goodness! What happened?

Social Worker: Sarah is okay, however she came to me earlier today and told me that she had been thinking about killing herself.

Mrs. Kline (crying): Oh my gosh! That's awful. Our little baby. Why would she say something like that?

Social Worker: I know this must be very difficult for you. I want you to know that I am here to answer and address all of your questions and concerns. This is a very serious matter, and I am here to offer you my support in any way I can.

Mrs. Kline: Thank you. I just can't believe she said that. She doesn't seem unhappy at home. Why didn't she come to us?

Social Worker: Sometimes children who are feeling sad or depressed hide it very well. They can even hide it from the people they love the most.

Mr. Kline: So, what should we do? Is she safe?

Social Worker: I conducted a suicide assessment on Sarah today, and based on the results shown here [shows parents the assessment], she is deemed a "low risk" as she does not have a specific plan of how she would harm herself. Even though Sarah did not have a specific plan, nor did she specify what she would use to do it, she did express that she has been thinking about suicide, and therefore we must do everything necessary to ensure her safety.

Mr. Kline: I agree.

Social Worker: I would not leave her alone at home for the next several days. At this time, I do not think Sarah is at imminent risk, as evidenced by the assessment tool, meaning I do not believe she will hurt herself tonight. However, I would advise you that if you are fearing for her safety tonight or any other night, you should call 911 or take her to your local emergency room. I want to provide you with the appropriate steps to take in case Sarah does express a desire to hurt herself. I have also provided Sarah with a "No Harm Contract" [see p. 21] in which she has agreed to tell a trusted adult if she has thoughts of hurting herself.

Mrs. Kline: Thank you very much. We will watch her for sure. This is all so upsetting.

Social Worker: I can imagine that this must be very difficult for you. I want you to know that this is not your fault and that Sarah is lucky to have such caring parents. I would like to offer some referrals for outside therapists for Sarah, as she may benefit from some therapy to help her deal with her feelings of sadness.

Mrs. Kline: We would gladly accept any referrals that will help Sarah. We just want to make sure she is happy!

This is a short snippet of an example of how a meeting with the parents of a suicidal child may go. Notice that the social worker allows the parents to express their feelings regarding the news. The social worker acknowledges the difficulty of the news and takes the opportunity to educate the parents about how adolescents who are feeling suicidal may hide their feelings from their parents. However, the social worker always remains on task and creates a plan of action. The social worker shows the parents the assessment tool used to conduct a suicide assessment on their child. This helps to back up the statements of the social worker and provides concrete information for the parents, who may be in denial about the risk of a suicidal child. Although the social worker states their feeling that the student is a "low risk," as proven by the results of the assessment tool, they still provide the parents with referrals and information about what to do if their child becomes a threat to herself. Even in situations when you do not feel a child is in any danger, *always* provide parents with options of what to do after school hours. Ultimately, the social worker offers guidance, support, and recommendations, but it is up to the parents what actions they take. Also note that the social worker did not make a diagnosis of depression but simply stated that Sarah may be experiencing feelings of sadness. It is up to the parents now to take their daughter to a professional outside of school to get properly diagnosed.

• • •

Note: The examples in this chapter are to provide you with effective communication techniques in talking with parents about sensitive topics. They are not meant to provide you with protocols for how to handle certain situations. In fact, many of the issues covered, such as suicide and bullying, would also require the involvement of an administrator, especially if disciplinary action were necessary. More often than not, in certain situations, your administrator may be present at your initial meeting with a parent or parents. There also may be school policy or protocol that will need to be discussed during your meetings with parents. In no way am I suggesting that you simply meet with the parents of a student who is bullying others, for example, and that will be the end of it. As I state throughout this book, I am simply providing you with guidelines and examples of how to handle certain situations that you can then take and adjust to meet the needs of the students at your school. Just remember, effective communication encompasses empathy, support, and nonjudgment. It is all about how you approach the situation!

Chapter 7

CRISIS INTERVENTION— PROTOCOLS AND ASSESSMENTS

This chapter explores and provides you with the necessary knowledge and tools to deal with crisis intervention to help you in the creation of effective school policies and child abuse reports and to understand the limits of confidentiality. The tools in this section include an explanation of confidentiality and its limits; suicide, homicide, and substance abuse protocols; and information on how to conduct an assessment in these situations. A "how-to" guide for when and how to report a case of child abuse as a mandated reporter is also included.

CONFIDENTIALITY

Confidentiality and the limits to it for you, as a school social worker, can pose ethical dilemmas. Many students enjoy coming to their school social worker so that they can share their innermost feelings and thoughts without the fear that their parents will be told everything they reveal in counseling. School social workers are bound by law to break confidentiality in several instances, but they are also limited in confidentiality due to the fact that they work in schools and with minor children.

Although most information between a social worker and student remains confidential, several limitations exist. Many schools now place additional limits on confidentiality, such as the required reporting of the use of illegal drugs, all sexual activity of students under the age of 17, all teen pregnancies, a list of all students receiving social work services, bullying incidents, and so on. These requirements vary between schools. The federal required limits to confidentiality are listed here.

LIMITS TO CONFIDENTIALITY FOR A SCHOOL SOCIAL WORKER

The contents of all counseling sessions are considered to be confidential. Neither verbal information nor written records about a client can be shared with another party without written consent of the client or the client's legal guardian. Noted exceptions are as follows:

Duty to Warn and Protect

When a client discloses intentions or a plan to harm another person, the mental health professional is required to warn the intended victim and report this information to legal authorities. In cases in which the client discloses or implies a plan for suicide, the mental health professional is required to notify legal authorities and make reasonable attempts to notify the family of the client.

Abuse of Children and Vulnerable Adults

If a client states or suggests that he or she is abusing a child (or vulnerable adult) or has recently abused a child (or vulnerable adult) or that a child (or vulnerable adult) is in danger of abuse, the mental health professional is required to report this information to the appropriate social service or legal authorities.

Prenatal Exposure to Controlled Substances

Mental health professionals are required to report admitted prenatal exposure to controlled substances that are potentially harmful.

Minors/Guardianship

Parents or legal guardians of nonemancipated minor clients have the right to access the clients' records (U.S. Department of Health and Human Services, Office of Civil Rights, n.d.; see also http://www.hhs.gov).

As mentioned previously, many schools are requiring school social workers to break confidentiality and report other incidents that are not necessarily required by law to be disclosed. Even if your school does not require you to break confidentiality in areas such as teen pregnancy, "sexting," or bullying, it may be wise to confide in your supervisor. If you ever feel uneasy about the information you receive, you should probably seek supervision or consultation regarding your feelings. Your job is to keep the students and the school safe. Sometimes, that means using your own discretion and breaking confidentiality.

TIP: According to federal education law (the Family Educational Rights and Privacy Act), any parent can request in writing or subpoena their child's records. This includes anything that their child's name appears on. This means your progress notes, incident reports, e-mails . . . everything! Be careful what you write! You should be brief and general when writing progress notes. If a student is over the age of 18, they too can request to see their files. A sure way to lose the trust of a student you are working with is having parents request their daughter's file, for example, and read in your progress notes that she is sexually active. You can just imagine how this would turn out, for you, the student, and the parents! Oh, and did I mention that your administrator would be involved?

TIP: It is usually best practice to discuss confidentiality during your initial meeting with a student. Tell them what confidentiality means and when it will be broken. When explaining the times it will be broken, during the child abuse explanation I also talk about statutory rape. You may be faced with a 15-year-old girl who is sexually active with an 18-year-old young man. This is considered statutory rape in many states and needs to be reported to Child Protective Services (CPS). Most adolescents do not understand this because the sex is often consensual. However, this is the law in many states, and this needs to be clearly explained to the adolescent you are working with.

Here is a sample of how I discuss confidentiality during my initial session:

"Hi. My name is_____. I am going to be your school social worker. Almost everything we talk about in my office will remain between us. That is called *confidentiality*. Confidentiality is just a big, fancy word that means what we say here stays here. However, there are some times that I will have to tell someone else about what we talk about in here. Those times include if you tell me that you want or have a plan to hurt yourself, hurt someone else, or are being abused by a parent or another person. They also include if you are in a sexual relationship with a person over the age of 18. This is considered statutory rape, and I have to report that as child abuse. I also will have to tell someone if you come to session under the influence of drugs and/or alcohol. It is my job to keep you safe, and I can't keep those things to myself.

"Additionally, there may be times that I think it may benefit you if we tell someone else about what we talk about in here. For example, if you tell me you are having a really difficult time in math class, I may suggest that we tell your math teacher about your concerns. However, I will *always* talk to you about it first and will not go behind your back without your permission. Deal?

"How does that sound to you? Do you have any questions? Do you understand what confidentiality is and when it needs to be broken?"

Discuss the student's concerns and questions regarding confidentiality.

You may also want to include in your discussion how confidentiality will be broken when speaking with the student's parents. You can tell them that you may speak to their parents but that you will keep their information confidential, with the exceptions of the limitations that you already discussed. This is extremely important if you are working with adolescents, because often they don't want their parents to know anything about them! Assure the adolescent that you will keep their information private, but that you may need to speak to their parents at times and will be general in what you tell them.

CRISIS INTERVENTION—PROTOCOLS AND ASSESSMENTS

In the event that a student threatens to harm themselves or others, immediate, appropriate, and precise intervention should occur. A policy or protocol should be established within your school to effectively deal with these types of crisis situations. It is extremely important that your policy include assessment, intervention, and follow-up components. Having all three pieces will help ensure the safety of the student, which is primary, but it will also protect you as the school social worker, the school, and your license against law suits and other legal actions that could occur in a situation of crisis. Although ensuring the safety of the student during the crisis is the immediate need, the follow-up component to a crisis situation is just as important. So, if your risk assessment points to a high risk and a psychiatric hospitalization is necessary, make sure that a plan is also put into place after the student is released from the hospital and returns to school. Often school social workers take the necessary action to ensure the safety of a student initially but neglect to follow up after the crisis is resolved.

Detailed crisis intervention protocols and assessments are provided in this section. Remember that after completing an assessment and crisis intervention, you should *always* document what happened on an incident report form or another form of documentation required by your school. I can't stress enough how important documentation is in situations of crisis.

Note: In times of crisis intervention or risk of suicide or homicide, you may feel overwhelmed and stressed. It is important that you contact your administrator and not attempt to handle the crisis alone. In addition, after the crisis has been handled, it may be beneficial for you, administration, and all staff involved to meet to process the incident.

Ultimately, we are no help to anyone if we do not help ourselves first! Don't forget about self-care!

Suicide Threat

When a student threatens suicide, the following protocol should be followed:

At no time should the student making the threat of suicide be left unattended. If there is a time that the student must be left alone in an office, the door should be left open and an adult should be able to see the student at all times. The student should never be unattended at any time.

1. The student who made the threat should be immediately sent to the school social worker.
2. The school social worker will perform an assessment that will determine the risk of suicide on a scale of low, medium, or high (see p. 170).
3. The school social worker will inform their administrator after completion of the assessment.
4. The administrator or school social worker will call the student's parents to come in for a meeting as soon as possible.
5. The parents will be informed of the suicide threat regardless of level of risk.
6. The parents will be given referrals for outpatient services for low and medium levels of risk.

The following steps should be followed in the event the assessment reveals a high level of risk:

7. The parents of the student will be informed of the high risk of suicidality. The parents will be urged to take their child to the nearest emergency room for a psychiatric evaluation. Referrals will be given for hospitals.
8. A release of information consent form should be given to the parent to sign so that the school can communicate with the hospital to ensure that service needs are met.

After the parent takes the student to the emergency room, the parent or hospital will be required (with the parent's consent) to send paperwork stating that the child is no longer a threat to themselves or others and is clear to return to school. This

SUICIDE RISK ASSESSMENT

NAME: _____   DATE: _____

SCHOOL: _____

1. Have you ever thought of committing suicide? OR Are you thinking of killing yourself?

    If the answer is yes, continue with the rest of the assessment questions. If the answer is no, assess for prevalent risk factors, such as feelings of worthlessness, hopelessness, apathy, loss of interest in things that used to be interesting, sadness, tearfulness, loss or gain in appetite, insomnia or too much sleeping, or a desire to disappear or go away forever.

2. How often have you had these thoughts?

3. Has anything happened recently to make you feel like this?

4. On a scale of 1 to 10, how strong is the desire to kill yourself?

5. What would it take to move down one point on the scale?

6. Have you ever thought how you would kill yourself?

7. Have you ever tried anything like that before? What happened?

8. Do you have the means to enact this plan? (Examples: easy access to bullets, pills, a gun, or a knife.)

Low Risk: No current plan, no major risk factors.

Medium Risk: General plan but no intent to act on this current plan. No history of attempted suicide or no current plan, but some major risk factors exist.

High Risk: Current plan and lethal means available. History of attempts or current plan with major risk factors present.

Indicate Risk: Low   Medium   High

paperwork will be kept by the school social worker, the administrator, and the registrar for attendance purposes.

In the case of a high risk of suicide revealed by the assessment and a noncompliant parent, the school must *immediately call CPS, followed by the police. The police should be notified if a student is deemed a high risk for suicide and the administration of the school does not feel that the student is going to receive the adequate help that they need. If the school feels that the student is a danger to themselves or others, the police should be notified as well as CPS due to neglect of the parent to provide immediate medical attention.*

Homicide Threat or Threat of Violence

When a student threatens homicide or harm to another person, the following protocol should be followed:

1. The student who made the threat should be immediately referred to administration. (This includes a threat of violence in any form, such as a threat to fight, a threat to bring a weapon to school, or a threat to harm any other student by force or violence.)
2. Administration will contact the school social worker to perform an assessment to determine level of risk as low, medium, or high (see p. 172).
3. The administrator or school social worker will call the student's parents to come in for a meeting.
4. The parents will be notified of the threat regardless of level of risk.
5. The parents will be given referrals for low and medium levels of risk.
6. The administration will determine a disciplinary consequence for the homicide or violence threat.

The following protocol should be followed in the event the assessment reveals a high level of risk:

7. The parents of the student will be informed of the high risk of homicidality. The parents will be urged to take their child to the nearest emergency room for a psychiatric evaluation. Referrals will be given for hospitals.
8. A release of information consent form should be given to the parent to sign so that the school can communicate with the hospital to ensure that service needs are met.

After the parent takes the student to the emergency room, the parent or hospital will be required (with the parent's consent) to send paperwork stating the child is no

HOMICIDE/THREAT OF VIOLENCE RISK ASSESSMENT

NAME: _____ DATE: _____

SCHOOL: _____

1.   Have you ever thought about hurting or killing someone else?

     If the answer is yes, continue with the rest of the assessment questions. If the answer is no, assess for prevalent risk factors, such as anger, lack of remorse, apathy, loss of interest in things that used to be interesting, rage, tearfulness, violent gestures, inability to calm down, history of erratic or violent behavior, history of suspensions, expulsions, or immense amount of behavioral problems.

2.   How often have you had these thoughts?

3.   Has anything happened recently to make you want to hurt someone?

4.   On a scale of 1 to 10, how strong is your desire to hurt someone?

5.   What would it take to move you down one point on the scale?

6.   Have you ever thought about how you would hurt someone? When?

7.   Do you have the means to enact this plan?

8.   Have you ever done anything like this before?

Low Risk: No current plan, no major risk factors.

Medium Risk: General plan but no intent to act on this current plan. No history of attempted homicide or no current plan, but some major risk factors exist.

High Risk: Current plan and lethal means available. History of attempts or current plan with major risk factors present. History of or current violent behavior.

Indicate Risk: Low   Medium   High

longer a threat to themselves or others and is clear to return to school. This paperwork will be kept by the school social worker, the administrator, and the registrar for attendance purposes.

In the case of a high risk of homicide revealed by the assessment and a noncompliant parent, the school must *immediately call CPS, followed by the police. The police should be notified if a student is deemed a high risk for homicide and the administration of the school does not feel that the student is going to receive the adequate help that they need. If the school feels that the student is a danger to themselves or others, the police should be notified as well as CPS due to neglect of the parent to provide immediate medical attention.*

Illegal Substance Use/Abuse or Possession

The following protocol should be followed if a student is in possession or under the influence of an illegal substance:

1. The student will immediately be referred to administration.
2. The school social worker will be called in to offer assessment and recommendations. (No formal assessment for safety needs to be conducted unless the student threatens harm to themselves or others.)
3. The student's parents will be called and informed about the possession or use of illegal substances.
4. Administration will determine disciplinary consequences.
5. Referrals will be given for counseling/rehabilitation services.

Return to School after Psychiatric Hospitalization

All necessary staff and personnel should be informed about the hospitalization of any student while abiding by confidentiality and Health Insurance Portability and Accountability Act laws. Necessary staff and personnel include school administration, the school social worker, the registrar, necessary teachers, and Special Education Department staff. This will ensure that the correct action is taken in setting up services, such as counseling, behavioral interventions, classroom accommodations, and so on.

A plan to integrate the student back into school will be formulated and decided on by the administration, school social worker, and teachers involved.

HOW AND WHEN TO REPORT CHILD ABUSE

As a school professional, you are a *mandated* reporter and *must* report all suspicions of child abuse to CPS within 24 hours of your knowledge of the suspected abuse. If you do *not* do this, you could lose your job and your license and even face jail time. My advice to you is this: Even if you aren't sure if a student is a victim of abuse, make the call to CPS. CPS will either take the case and investigate for alleged abuse or close the case for a lack of evidence supporting a finding of abuse. It is *not* your job to determine whether a child is being abused or not. It is just your job to call CPS.

To become licensed as a social worker, you must have completed a child abuse reporting course. However, this course is usually conducted during one's MSW program and often not refreshed in the workplace. So, depending on where you are employed, you may not be faced with a child abuse case for several years after you took the child abuse reporting course. This section provides you with a quick and easy guide to know how and when to report child abuse. The signs of potential abuse are also included.

There are four main types of abuse: physical abuse, sexual abuse, emotional maltreatment, and neglect.

Signs of Physical Abuse

Consider the possibility of physical abuse when the child:

- Has unexplained burns, bites, bruises, broken bones, or black eyes
- Has fading bruises or other marks noticeable after an absence from school
- Seems frightened of the parents and protests or cries when it is time to go home
- Shrinks at the approach of adults
- Reports injury by a parent or another adult caregiver

Signs of Sexual Abuse

Consider the possibility of sexual abuse when the child:

- Has difficulty walking or sitting
- Suddenly refuses to change for gym or to participate in physical activities
- Reports nightmares or bedwetting
- Experiences a sudden change in appetite
- Demonstrates bizarre, sophisticated, or unusual sexual knowledge or behavior
- Becomes pregnant or contracts a venereal disease, particularly if under age 14
- Runs away
- Reports sexual abuse by a parent or another adult caregiver

Signs of Emotional Maltreatment

Consider the possibility of emotional maltreatment when the child:

- Shows extremes in behavior, such as overly compliant or demanding behavior, extreme passivity, or aggression
- Is either inappropriately adult (parenting other children, for example) or inappropriately infantile (frequently rocking or head-banging, for example)
- Is delayed in physical or emotional development
- Has attempted suicide
- Reports a lack of attachment to the parent

Signs of Neglect

Consider the possibility of neglect when the child:

- Is frequently absent from school
- Begs or steals food or money
- Lacks needed medical or dental care, immunizations, or glasses
- Is consistently dirty and has severe body odor
- Lacks sufficient clothing for the weather
- Abuses alcohol or other drugs
- States that there is no one at home to provide care

(*Source:* Child Welfare Information Gateway, 2007)

Reporting

You, as a school social worker, are a mandated reporter. If you recognize the signs of abuse or neglect, you are required to report these. So, how do you report it?

When to Report

There are several different ways in which you may be faced with having to make a report to CPS:

1. A child may disclose abuse to you during a counseling session. Again, it is *not* your job to determine whether abuse exists or not. Often, social workers want to probe the child for more information about the abuse. Although you will be asking questions so that you have enough information for CPS, remember that you are *not* the CPS investigator, you are only the reporter. In a case in which a child discloses to you that they are being abused, you should

call immediately. Depending on the extent of the abuse, an alternative plan to sending the child home may have to be put into place. CPS will help you with this.

TIP: If your school doesn't already have a policy in place about who to notify when there is a suspected child abuse case, you may want to implement one. You are a mandated reporter and *must* call CPS to report any suspected abuse or neglect, but it is also a good idea to inform your principal or supervisor.

Mandated reporting is anonymous, but more often than not parents and caregivers figure out that the school was the source of the call. You can and *should* expect a call or visit from a parent as soon as CPS notifies them of the allegation of suspected abuse. If the parent shows up at your school, it is a good idea to have informed your principal that you made the call so that you can get support when talking with the parent. Remember, even if the parent assumes it was you who made the call, you do *not* have to confirm that you made the call if you do not want to. CPS reporting is anonymous!

In the past, however, I have found (in select cases) that it can be quite therapeutic in working with the parent to disclose that you are the one who reported to CPS. Often this allows you to educate the parent about what abuse and neglect are and that you are a mandated reporter. In a country full of so many different cultures and ethnicities, many parents lack education regarding our child abuse laws. By providing them with the correct information, you can perhaps prevent future child abuse or neglect. Ideally, this conversation with the parent would happen before a call to CPS has to be made, but that cannot always be the case.

2. A teacher or staff member comes to you and reports that a student told them that they were being abused. Again, depending on the policy of the school, you may want to bring the student into your office and ask them a few questions regarding the alleged abuse. Remember that these questions are only to get enough information to report to the CPS investigator. Also, tell the teacher or staff member who reported the abuse to you that they also *must* call CPS. In other words, in this case, you *and* the other staff member will call CPS. *Every* mandated reporter who has knowledge about suspected abuse *must* report it to CPS within 24 hours.

You may have to help the teacher or staff member in making the report. It might be the first time they have ever reported, and most likely they will not be as well versed in the reporting process as you are. In addition, your administrator or principal should be informed about the situation if they have not already been made aware of it.

3. A student comes to you and reports that one of their friends is being abused. This is a very tricky situation, because often abuse is defined differently by a child. A six-year-old may think that being spanked once is child abuse, whereas a 14-year-old may think that their mother is abusing them by taking away their cell phone. Either way, it is best to try and find out more information.

    Be careful here! Most likely the student who came to you to tell you about the abuse is afraid that their friend will be mad at them for telling. Assure the student that you will *not* tell the other student that they were the one to tell you but that you *must* talk to the other student about the alleged abuse. When speaking with the student who is suspected of being abused, proceed as you would if the student themselves revealed the alleged abuse to you.

    Note: Sometimes a student will deny the abuse altogether and wonder where you got the idea that they are being abused. This makes your job very difficult. My advice is to look for signs that tell you the student may be being abused and to trust your intuition. If you feel something isn't right, *make the call*. I can't emphasize this enough: You would rather be safe than sorry! If you are wrong and make the call and there is no abuse, then great! But if you don't make the call and something happens, you will be in a lot of legal trouble, not to mention the ethical turmoil you will face.

I am addressing this book to school social workers and am not suggesting that you call CPS every five minutes because a student told you that their mother or father spanked them once or slapped their hand when they were five. I trust you know yourself and have good background knowledge regarding what abuse is and is not. This should serve simply as a refresher course and resource for those in need.

How to Report

Reporting laws vary from state to state, but most require that you either call in, mail in, or fill out a report online, and some require some combination of the three. To find out about your state laws regarding reporting child abuse as a mandated reporter, visit the Child Welfare Information Gateway: http://www.childwelfare.gov. The National Child Abuse Reporting Hotline is 1-800-4-A-CHILD.

What Happens after the Report

Probably the most frustrating feeling after a social worker reports suspected abuse to CPS is not knowing what will happen. Unfortunately, you may never find out what happens after a call to CPS is made. CPS investigators are under no obligation to report back to the social worker the findings of a case. Social workers are able to tell the CPS investigator (or check off a box if reporting online) that they want to be notified of any case findings, but more often than not you will not be contacted. If a CPS case remains open, most school social workers will hear from the CPS caseworker assigned to the case. The caseworker will call and ask about the attendance and behavior of the student. You *must* give the requested information to the CPS caseworker. Child abuse is a limit to confidentiality (see the "Limits to Confidentiality for a School Social Worker" section earlier in this chapter), and no parental consent for release of information is needed. However, many school social workers do eventually find out what happens after the CPS call is made, simply because they are in the school and have daily access to students. In my experience, often either the student themselves, a sibling, or a friend tells me what happened without my even asking.

• • •

I hope that I have provided you with a helpful resource regarding identifying and reporting child abuse. Please remember, though, that this is only an overview of how and when to report suspected child abuse. For a more thorough explanation about mandated reporting, see http://www.childwelfare.gov.

Chapter 8

FORMS AND OTHER USEFUL TOOLS

This chapter includes forms and other useful tools for the school social worker. Forms previously discussed and presented in the book are not included in this chapter (though there is a handy guide to where they can be found), but some additional forms are. Forms that can be found in this section include a sample parental consent form, a sign-in sheet, progress note and treatment plan forms, and a social worker/counselor newsletter.

WHERE TO FIND FORMS IN
THE SCHOOL SOCIAL WORK TOOLKIT

SCHOOL SOCIAL WORKER NEWSLETTER

Communication between a school social worker and administrative staff is not only important, it's imperative for the effectiveness of the school social worker's job. However, school social workers and school administrators are often very busy and only have time for five-minute check-ins on a daily basis. A counselor/social worker newsletter can serve as an effective and efficient communication tool between the school social worker and school administrator or principal. The newsletter can be weekly or monthly. This letter is meant to enhance communication between the school social worker and the administrative staff. It is meant for intraschool communication only. However, a parent newsletter is always a good idea as well.

The school newsletter can include ideas and suggestions that the social worker has as well as groups and workshops the social worker is running or wants to implement. Updates on cases and daily duties can be included as well, such as mediations that occurred, counseling sessions, conflict resolution sessions, parent meetings, and so on. This is a great way to inform your school administrator what has been going on without taking up too much time and to create some job security for yourself by showing all that you do (which we all know is *a lot!*).

Note: It is important to note that crisis interventions *can* be included in the newsletter but only after the social worker has spoken with the administrator. In other words, if a crisis intervention is mentioned in the newsletter, this should not be the first time the administrator is hearing about it. Also, remember that everything that goes in the newsletter needs to preserve confidentiality, so leaving out names and descriptive factors is a must. (See the sample newsletter beginning on the next page for an idea of how to write one. It is an example of a newsletter that I sent out weekly to my administrators in the elementary, middle, and high school of the district I worked in.)

COUNSELOR'S CORNER NEWSLETTER

Hello [School Name] Administrators:

This newsletter is to provide you with an overview of each week in the counseling world at [School Name] as well as to offer suggestions and plans for the future. Please offer feedback, suggestions, and criticisms to me via e-mail or personal contact. I will be following up with each of you in the future so that we can all be on the same page. Thanks so much for your continued support.

Week ending [Date]

WHAT'S GOING ON AT [SCHOOL NAME]??

ELEMENTARY SCHOOL:

Groups Currently Running:

4th–5th Grade Girls Group:

Led therapeutic activity using art materials, dealing with antibullying, and social skills strategies.

Students used art materials to portray ways to handle peer-pressure situations.

K–2nd Grade Boys Group:

Led social skill-building exercise. Group worked together to reach a common goal.

4th–5th Grade Boys Group:

Led anger management activity. Students learned healthy ways to manage their anger and make good choices. A collage was made using art materials.

COUNSELOR'S CORNER NEWSLETTER (CONTINUED)

Individual Cases (Case Highlights):

1st grader—Student continues to show sadness but has not made statements regarding dying or death in the last 2.5 weeks. (This is an update from the meeting we had regarding this student as it was deemed a crisis situation.)

4th grader—Met with principal and staff to determine next steps for behavior management. Academic and psychological testing recommended.

5th grader—Added a new student to caseload to receive counseling services due to past trauma (deceased mother) and current peer difficulties.

Incident of bullying reported in 4th and 5th grades. Met with administration and teachers to resolve conflict and with parents of all students involved.

Teachers:

Led professional development workshop on "Tips for Teachers Working with Difficult Students."

Parent Conferences:

Parent conferences are going well! I offered tips and strategies for healthy parenting as well as how to handle behavior and stress during state exam time.

Test Anxiety Workshops:

I have completed three workshops in the elementary school thus far. Workshops are going well! The kids are using the techniques and reporting less anxiety toward testing. Workshops to continue for next two weeks.

MIDDLE SCHOOL:

Groups Currently Running:

6th–8th Grade Boys Group:

Led a discussion and lecture regarding how to be successful at [School Name]. Spoke about keeping a planner and creating relationships with peers, administrators, counselors, and teachers. [School Name] Code of Conduct reviewed.

COUNSELOR'S CORNER NEWSLETTER (CONTINUED)

Individual Cases:

Added two new cases to my caseload for test anxiety counseling. Counseling will be short term and solution focused to teach students coping strategies to deal with test anxiety.

Test Anxiety Workshops:

Workshops are going well! The kids are using the techniques and reporting less anxiety toward testing. Workshops to continue for next two weeks.

Parent Conferences:

Parent conferences going well! I offered tips and strategies for healthy parenting as well as how to handle behavior and stress during state exam time.

Met with several parents to suggest that their children be brought to the attention of the Student Support Team Committee for determination of services and/or psychological testing.

HIGH SCHOOL:

Groups Currently Running:

9th–11th Grade Boys Group/Anger Management:

Led a discussion and lecture regarding how to be successful at [School Name]. Spoke about keeping a planner and creating relationships with peers, administrators, counselors, and teachers. [School Name] Code of Conduct reviewed.

Peer Mediation:

Continued eight-week training. Steps 3–6 covered in six-step peer mediation training.

Individual Cases:

9th grader—Met with Student Support Team about student. Student is currently failing several classes. Student's parents were contacted and attended meeting. Student to begin receiving, tutoring, counseling, and homework hall services. Student will be recommended for special education testing. Parents are supportive and in agreement with school for testing recommendation. School social worker to continue organization and

COUNSELOR'S CORNER NEWSLETTER (CONTINUED)

social skills work on an individual basis through counseling. Special education testing to be scheduled with school psychologist.

10th grader—Added a new student to my caseload to receive counseling services for symptoms of depression and a possible eating disorder. Student to receive counseling services in school, with a possible future referral for outside services.

Parent Conferences:

Parent conferences completed at high school level. Several students referred for Student Support Team for review and discussion.

Teachers:

Led professional development for teachers on how to build and maintain relationships with difficult students.

PLANS/SUGGESTIONS:

Sex Ed Class: I have met with the school nurse and health education teacher and begun discussion about implementing a sexual education class. Ideas to be discussed with administrator in near future.

Suicide Awareness Workshops for Students: I would like to begin implementing a workshop on suicide prevention as next month is Suicide Awareness Month. Let's chat!

CRISIS INTERVENTION AND FOLLOW-UP:

Child Protective Services report was made for a 7th grade student for alleged physical abuse. Caseworker will follow up directly with me, per my request. Met with administration and sent documentation about this case previously.

10th grade student hospitalized for suicide attempt at home. Met with parent and obtained a release of information to speak with the hospital. Waiting to hear back from the hospital regarding the student's progress and status.

Bullying incident between three 9th grade girls. Met with administration and parents previously to resolve conflict and will continue to monitor the situation by speaking with the students and their families.

PARENTAL CONSENT FOR COUNSELING SERVICES

In keeping with the state education laws, please offer your parental consent by signing the attached form and returning it to the school social worker so that your child has access to [School Name]'s guidance and counseling services.

I hereby give my consent for my child, _____,
to receive services from the [School Name]'s guidance and counseling services.

I hereby DO NOT give consent for my child, _____,
to receive services from the [School Name]'s guidance and counseling services.

Parent/Guardian Signature _____

SIGN-IN SHEET

DATE	PERIOD/TIME	NAME (PLEASE PRINT)

INDIVIDUAL PROGRESS NOTES

Name of Student _____

DATE and TIME	NOTE

GROUP PROGRESS NOTES

Name of Group _____

Names/Initials of Students_____

DATE and TIME	NOTE

[SCHOOL NAME] TREATMENT PLAN

Name of Student _____Date _____

Diagnosis (optional as many school social workers do not or cannot diagnose students):

Axis I _____

Axis II _____

Axis III _____

Axis IV _____

Axis V _____ (GAF)

Symptoms prior to beginning counseling: _____

_____

_____

Medical problems/medication: _____

_____

People living in household: _____

_____

Abuse history/CPS involvement: _____

_____

Treatment goals: _____

_____

_____

REFERENCES
AND RESOURCES

Australian Government Department of Health and Aging. (2006). *A review of the research to identify the most effective models of practice in early intervention with autism spectrum disorders.* Retrieved from http://www.health.gov.au/internet/publications/publishing.nsf/Content/mental-child-autrev-toc

Child Welfare Information Gateway. (2007). *Recognizing child abuse and neglect: Signs and symptoms.* Retrieved from http://www.childwelfare.gov/pubs/factsheets/signs.cfm

Edwin Gould Services for Children and Families. (n.d.). *Relationship Abuse Prevention Program (RAPP).* Retrieved from http://www.egscf.org/services/steps/hra-relationship-abuse-prevention-program-rapp/

Epstein, M. (2000). The Behavioral and Emotional Rating Scale: A strength-based approach to assessment. *Assessment for Effective Intervention, 25,* 249–256.

Helpguide.org. (2012, April). *Domestic violence and abuse: Signs of abuse and abusive relationships.* Retrieved from http://www.helpguide.org/mental/domestic_violence_abuse_types_signs_causes_effects.htm

Inner Health Studio. (n.d.). *Relaxation examples.* Retrieved from http://www.innerhealthstudio.com/relaxation-examples.html

Microsoft Office Publisher (see http://office.microsoft.com/en-us/publisher/).

NASW Legal Defense Fund. (2011). *Client confidentiality and privileged communications.* Washington, DC: NASW Press.

National Institute of Mental Health. (2010, September 27). *Suicide in the U.S.: Statistics and prevention.* Retrieved from http://www.nimh.nih.gov/health/publications/suicide-in-the-us-statistics-and-prevention/index.shtml

New York State Office of Children and Family Services. (n.d.). *Child Protective Services.* Retrieved from http://www.ocfs.state.ny.us/main/cps/

Schrumpf, F., Crawford, D., & Bodine, R. (1997a). *Peer mediation conflict resolution in schools.* Champaign, IL: Research Press.

Schrumpf, F., Crawford, D., & Bodine, R. (1997b). *Peer mediation conflict resolution in schools: Student manual.* Champaign, IL: Research Press.

Simmons, R. (2002). *Odd girl out: The hidden culture of aggression in girls.* Boston: Houghton Mifflin Harcourt.

Simmons, R. (2004). *Odd girl speaks out: Girls write about bullies, cliques, popularity, and jealousy.* Boston: Houghton Mifflin Harcourt.

Statistic Brain. (n.d.). *High school dropout statistics.* Retrieved from http://www.statisticbrain.com/high-school-dropout-statistics

Students Against Violence Everywhere (SAVE) (see http://www.nationalsave.org).

Substance Abuse and Mental Health Services Administration. (2009, January 22). *Substance abuse and mental health statistics from SAMHSA's Office of Applied Studies (OAS).* Retrieved from http://oas.samhsa.gov/oasftp.cfm

Sunburst Visual Media. (1997). *Student workshop: Handling your anger.* Retrieved from http://www.ket.org/education/guides/selfmanagement/selfmanagement_prog12.pdf

Teaching Tolerance: A Project of the Southern Poverty Law Center (see http://www.tolerance.org/).

U.S. Department of Health and Human Services, Office of Civil Rights. (n.d.). *Understanding health information privacy.* Retrieved from http://www.hhs.gov/ocr/privacy/hipaa/understanding/index.html

Volkmar, F. R., & Wiesner, L. A. (2009). *A practical guide to autism: What every parent, family member, and teacher needs to know.* Hoboken, NJ: John Wiley & Sons.

Weisenger, H. (1985). *Dr. Weisinger's anger work-out book: Step-by-step methods for greater productivity, better relationships, healthier life.* New York: William Morrow.

Wiseman, R. (2009). *Queen bees and wannabes: Helping your daughter survive cliques, gossip, boyfriends, and the new realities of girl world.* New York: Three Rivers Press.

INDEX

Page numbers in **bold** denote forms or documentation.

HAIRSTON 07 OCT 2020